Little Brown Boots

Down a Rabbit Hole

Valerie Schram–Bolen

Tellwell Talent
www.tellwell.ca

ISBN
978-0-2288-2522-7 (Hardcover)
978-0-2288-2521-0 (Paperback)
978-0-2288-2523-4 (eBook)

Praise for Little Brown Boots

An historical love story by Valerie Bolen – Transparent Perception of a Canadian Heart

Honoured to edit numerous autobiographies, the story so openly expressed in "Little Brown Boots" triggered me emotionally in the first pages. Beyond measure, a widow's description of the profound heart love and dedication shared with her husband, Carl, is romantically inspirational. The truth of the realities of family, friends, hopes, daily joys, humour and challenges are also written without bias or resentment by Valerie Bolen. She recreates memories back to the era before Canada's involvement in World War II to our 21st Century technical world, taking readers even deeper. The challenges of working with gifts of nature, abiding by local and company rules in Northern Ontario communities are historical lessons we never learned in school. It might take a movie to stir the tears I swallowed back as this story unfolded. Well…why not?

Judy Watts, BA
Author, Editor, Former College Professor
wattsjudy04@gmail.com

What I value most in this unique heartwarming story is how Valerie brought the truth to light. Writing her story by hand, sharing such emotional loss, proves how she always trusts the best in people.

I can verify the wonderful chemistry in her marriage through the loving sparkle in Carl's eyes when the family regularly came for a weekend dinner to The Café. He would sit quietly while his blue eyes emitted such joy, as he observed and observed, treasuring everything in his vision.

I was privileged to know Valerie even more over the years once we became back door neighbors. And when we worked together, as she managed The Café for me, I truly appreciated her outlook on life and love and commitment.

This publication will be kind of those special stories readers will remember and share. Thank you, Valerie, for your insight and inspiration. You are always in my heart.

Cherie A. Carpenter

TABLE OF CONTENTS

DEDICATION AND PREFACE

When thinking of all the special people who are close to my heart who I would be proud to dedicate my work to, my father and sister come to the front of the line.

In most cases, dedications are short and to the point. In reading mine, you will find it to be unusual. I am offering insight into my father's childhood that I feel compelled to pass on to you, the reader. It will give you a clearer vision as to why I chose him, as well as my sister, to dedicate my work to. This is by no means to take away from my story of Carl. It is to enlighten you to the tragedy suffered by my father at an early age, along with the heartache felt by both Carl and me with the loss of my sister, Diane. My father overcame his challenges through his love of reading, finding a comfort and peace in the books he read.

My father was Sydney Jay Schram. He was born on November 14, 1918, and left us on December 28, 2001. He was an avid reader, taking an empty cardboard box along on his trips to the town library, bringing it home full of books for his enjoyment. It got to the point where, having read all the books in the library, he couldn't find anything new to read! Often, he would have two books on the go at the same time. When he knew Carl and I were planning a trip to Stratton, he never failed to call to ask if I had any reading material to bring along. I believe he was a "self-taught" man with beautiful handwriting, excellent math skills and, of course, an addiction to reading.

After losing his mother, Gladys Pauline Foe-Schram, who died at the young age of twenty-seven years old from diphtheria, his life was never the same. He was three years old at the time with a sister, Thelma Gladys, who was five years old, and a little brother, Harry

Leslie, who was only fourteen months old. They were sent down east to the Hamilton area to live as their father couldn't farm and care for three small children. Sydney and Thelma were to live with an aunt, while Harry was sent to another aunt's house, the aunts being sisters of their mother. Harry passed away at the tender age of two years and nine months old from loneliness, according to my father.

My grandmother, a schoolteacher at the time of her illness, was teaching at Pattullo #8 school. If memory serves me correctly, my father once told me that he only attended school until Grade 4. He certainly would have made his mother proud of his academic skills and love of reading, which was passed down to his children and later to his grandchildren.

To dedicate my writings to him would be a great honour—he would be so proud of my accomplishments. I, along with my siblings, thought of him as our *"book of knowledge."* He was always there for us with an answer to any question we had.

Along with this dedication to my father, I must also dedicate my writing to my sister, Diane Frances Schram-Nordin. My beautiful, bubbly sister made the sun shine even on cloudy days with her sparkling personality and outstanding smile. Diane lost her life far too early in a tragic automobile/train accident just east of Rainy River on January 19, 1994. January is the month of winter when the weather is cold and the country roads icy. She had just celebrated her 35th birthday on January 10. She left behind her husband, Tim, and their four babies, all girls: Lindsey, Alicia, Kayla, and Carling. She would be so proud of the young women they are today, and is now guiding them from heaven with all the love she showered on them when she was here. As well, she is sending down her love to the grandchildren she now has, and would be so delighted with them, keeping a watchful eye from above. During her years, she was also an avid reader like most of her siblings, gifted with this love from our father.

This one is for you, Daddy and Diane. Enjoy! Love, your girl and sister, Valerie Gladys Schram Bolen.

Daddy and Diane

Daddy and Diane

INTRODUCTION

This is my first attempt at writing, getting this need of mine out of my bucket list. It has been in there for a good many years. As you know, I am no longer the "youngest bunny" in the coop. My "fur" is now a winter white rather than the pretty brown it used to be back in the day.

Also, I can't forget that I was once called "Old Lady," a comment that jarred me into taking a second look at myself, a comment that I'm still having trouble with. I can sort of tell from the signs, though, that there may be some truth here: writer's cramp, writer's block, and now this new thing—swollen legs from sitting too long while writing.

Enough about me and my signs of aging. My husband, Carl, is my main reason for writing this story. I don't think he would mind too much what I have shared with you. He was always an easygoing, kind, and gentle man. You will discover this when reading and following his story. During the course of my writing, I was to take a few sharp turns here and there—just like my granddaughter's pet miniature bunny that I was trying to chase down one day after it got loose outside. I was out of breath after this—much the same as Carl and I were after enjoying a polka.

I pretty much stripped him bare by the time I reached the end of his story. I apologize for that. There is nothing gracious about Alzheimer's disease. How you handle it makes a difference to the person suffering, crying out for help in the darkness on their journey *"down a rabbit hole."* Hold their hand, give them your love. I hope you enjoy reading my memories of Carl, the young man who left a mark on my heart those many years ago…who still held my hand until the end.

I won't forget you, Carl...

This is a favourite poem of ours, taken from a birthday card that I had given to Carl a few years earlier. We both enjoyed sitting on the deck when the lilacs were in full bloom, with butterflies enjoying the flowers as much as Carl and I did.

You will sit on the swing,
I will sit in the chair,
and the fragrance of lilacs
will hang in the air.
I will tell you a story
I've told you before.
We will laugh (like the last time)
and tell a few more.
Then perhaps we will say it,
and perhaps we will not,
but both our old hearts
will be thinking this thought—
That it's good to be known
and it's good to be there,
where the fragrance of lilacs
hangs in the air.

Carl's Little Brown Boots. Approximately 70 years old. They were on his feet for all of his journeys as a young boy, the soles completely worn through.

CHAPTER ONE

Seeing the Good

This is the story of a man's life. It is a story I would like to share with you from beginning to end, if I may. This man was my husband, the light of my life, my partner through good times and sad times, who took care of me and our family the best he could and never stopped smiling in the meantime. With Carl having been struck with Alzheimer's, I will be referring to a "rabbit hole" on occasion. This is the familiar path Alzheimer's takes on its course of destruction of mind and soul.

Carl was rather fond of foxes, having had a pet black fox years back when he worked at Brule Creek in the Huronian area. This fox napped in Carl's work truck during the day—Carl purposely left the door open for him. The fox was always happy to see him and would run up to him and try to climb up his legs when he arrived at work. A special lunch was packed in the lunch box every night so that they could enjoy their time together with a little picnic, just the two of them alone in the forest. This little fox had a "game" leg and Carl tried to make its life easier so it wouldn't have to search for food, giving its leg more time to heal.

This is just one of the ways in which Carl showed his kindness and caring for those less fortunate. In years to come, he never forgot to leave food along the roadside if we were on a trip past Brule Creek. Those beautiful little animals were known to have a den, a place to curl up in and raise their families, a cozy spot to offer them protection from the weather and predators.

Now then, a rabbit hole is underground and goes quite a distance with its twists and turns in the darkness before it comes back out into the daylight at the end of this tunnel which allows the rabbit to escape from foxes hungry for fresh rabbit for lunch. This journey with Carl reminded me of this, making me wonder if we were ever going to see daylight at the end of this particular tunnel. I longed for something to give us hope of getting out, get our feet back on the ground you might say, wipe the dirt off, dry our tears, and heal our battle scars (yes, there were a few of them). My reason for sharing this story is because Carl took me on quite a journey. And truth be told, I wouldn't have wanted to go on it with anyone else that I can think of right now.

It wasn't exactly a vacation by any means. There was no stopping on this trip—no pee-pee breaks or Planters peanuts, a favourite of his on a road trip. (Actually, this habit of eating peanuts annoyed me a bit, for you should always have both hands on the wheel and your eyes on the road ahead, and not be focussed on eating peanuts.) It's strange now that I'm thinking about it that we didn't have more bumps and bruising than what we had at the end of this journey, not to mention the deep scarring on my heart that I'm convinced isn't going to heal anytime soon.

Getting back to the beginning, fasten your seat belt for we are going on a road trip. It begins back a few years before they even had seat belts and inventions like that. It may have lessened some of the damage if we would have had back-up cameras back then, for they have proved to be a good thing it doesn't hurt to have.

Just to clear things up as you may begin to wonder about the condition of my mind or if maybe I should be medicated. I'll let you in on a little secret. I can quickly jump from one subject to another and change direction much like a rabbit when you least expect it...another good reason for the title of this tale. Anyway, I'm just warning you ahead of time in case I lose you for a minute. Maybe it comes with the old phrase, "aging gracefully." If you're like me and you don't speak quickly when a thought crosses your mind, you could possibly forget what you were thinking or talking about in the first place. I've had this happen on occasion and it can be quite embarrassing and just as

disturbing at the same time. It can get you thinking and wondering about your mind and the state it's in.

Now back to what I was saying about not wanting to go on this journey with anyone else but Carl. This is most likely due to the fact that we were married just shy of fifty-three years, not to mention the three to four years that I call our "learning" years before the ring came out of the glove box, as they called it back then.

Besides all this, Carl took good care of me during the course of our years together, once sitting up all night with me when I was in severe pain with a frozen shoulder. Also, I have to mention the great care he gave me when I had a severe nosebleed which was only from the right nostril. I couldn't move without it beginning to pour. After running back and forth to the emergency department for four days and being afraid after this length of time I was going to bleed to death, I rebelled! I refused to leave the hospital after having plugs put in to stop the bleeding because nothing seemed to work. I was beyond being afraid...I was scared senseless! I spent the night in our local hospital and the following day I was sent to Thunder Bay. We drove from Atikokan and our daughter Carla met us on the highway in case something went wrong. I was admitted into the Thunder Bay hospital where I spent the next seven days with a continuing nosebleed. After six plugs were put in and my blood pressure had spiked to 270 over 120, the doctor in charge decided to do exploratory surgery. He went above my teeth through the cheek bone and took a look around. He found the cause of my distress to be a ruptured artery. (The two clips he put on my artery to stop the bleeding are still in place today. These were used to reroute the blood flow.)

The following morning, they discharged me at 7 AM after 10 days of non-stop bleeding. I was so weak I could barely walk without help—and pale as a ghost. (Post-surgery my nose had to be repaired from all the plugs being inserted and removed!)

Carl was with me from morning to night helping me in any way he could. It was one of the most difficult times of my life. He was there for me with his gentle touch and caring ways. Thank you, Carl, for being there for me and for your gentleness and love. I know I have PTSD because there is not a day goes by that I don't check my nose several times for a bleed.

I am going to change paths again before I get too far ahead. This will be the start of making a rabbit hole come to life. After our fun years of courtship, starting our years together as young sweethearts, we should have had each other figured out, knowing in our hearts that we belonged together for the rest of our days. Growing old together was meant for us. We would take care of each other and still be smiling at the end.

I had my first glimpse of Carl when I may have been eleven or twelve years old, if that. He was at my grandparents' home and I was instantly struck by the gentle manner and kindness shown in how he treated the little children, cousins of mine who were at the farm visiting from out of town. I'm thinking he was there with his brother who was married to an aunt of mine. He surprised me with the respect that he showed the children. At this time, they were to be "seen and not heard," the old-fashioned way of raising families back then. Children were raised to not interrupt adults if they were visiting.

I look back on this encounter and know God had this planned for us for future reference. Returning to having each other figured out, it was a known fact that in our early years when Carl was in full courtship mode, we barely talked to each other. No words were needed. We had this knack of knowing what the other was thinking—telepathy, that's what it's known as. We were like two birds sitting on a farm fence, quietly enjoying each other's company. In our case, one look was all it took, and we knew what thoughts were crossing each other's mind. We didn't need lots of chirping and fluffing our feathers in our courtship or dance of love, if you choose to call it that. We danced to the beat of our own drum, pushed forward making our own path. It was special.

People wondered at the time how we could possibly get married, being we didn't talk much. We just knew in our hearts at that time that we were right for each other. As long as Carl's hand was holding mine, that's all I needed. I knew he was the one. He would always be there for me, keeping me safe and protected. I got this feeling just from his hand in mine. Yes, together we could face the world, he and I.

And after nearly fifty-three years of holding hands, we were still the same good friends as we were from the start. What more could a person want or ask for in their lifetime? All of the fun times we shared, the looks from those blue eyes. Oh, yes! I can't forget the beautiful smile that still got my heart beating a little bit faster whenever I looked his way.

Once much later on a road trip to Thunder Bay, we were stopped at a red light when a young lady crossed the street in front of our car. Jaycelin, our youngest granddaughter, made the comment: "Grandma, you'd better keep your eye on Grandpa. He's looking at that lady with love in his eyes." These were words of wisdom from a young girl which left me thinking, yes, Carl had that look of love on his face and wore it well. Always smiling, always melting my heart you might say. What more could I ask for than this? Starting out as an innocent farm girl, spending her days ahead with this young lad, breaking a path together in this game of life?

Getting back to the ring, I often wondered exactly how long it spent in the glove box. Maybe it would have been a good question to ask him. After all, I had plenty of time over the years. His big question was, "Do you want to try on a ring?" Of course, I did. And it fit! After this little episode, I went running into the house, waking up my mother to show her what had just happened to her girl. She said, "Well it's just about time."

Anyway, Carl and I didn't question each other too much. I guess we didn't invade each other's privacy—all part of paving the way to a good marriage. You just didn't question important happenings like that. One thing I did learn about Carl through the years of being together was that he liked to take his time when making big decisions, especially one as important as this one that was sure to change his life forever. The thought of going from being a carefree young man with few responsibilities to a married man most likely made him a bit fearful— this could take the fun out of things, to say the least. To top it off, he was easy to look at. Take my word for it! And, I was surely blessed that he had picked me. Those sparkling blue eyes and curly blond hair hanging over his forehead made this farm girl's heart beat a little bit faster.

Now I'm going to change course and slow down a bit here to the time before our big day and do a proper introduction of Carl. Being the "Boss" now, I'm going to tell you his story from the memories I've stored and the life I shared with him over the years. This new title of mine comes from the fact that when he had Alzheimer's, he needed me more than ever to look after him and protect him, so I became his official power of attorney. Later on, I will discuss this in more detail and explain what happened to bring this to light.

Yes, I was proud of this new job, and taking care of Carl would be my number one priority. In other words, to get to Carl, you would have to go through me—literally—which wasn't going to happen anytime soon. As long as I could still stand, I was here to protect him and keep him safe from harm and away from all the bull crap that seniors can encounter on a daily basis. (I don't know why people try to take advantage of those individuals with a bit of age showing on their faces. Just because we walk slowly doesn't mean we aren't as clever as we used to be. No, you can't fool us that easily and think we agree with everything we are told or hear. I guess you could say we've been around the block a few times and most of us have learned a thing or two during this trip.)

There were days when keeping Carl safe was challenging, for trouble seemed to hide around every corner waiting to pounce on him like a playful kitten, but the end results were to be more painful. The chore of trying to prevent him from falling was to be a job unto itself, for breaking a hip could mean the end for sure—as he had been told.

To start from the beginning, my sweetheart was born in his family home in Shenston, which is in the Chapple district, north of the Barwick-Stratton line. We both liked the sounds of that. Being that I was from Stratton, an honourable mention wouldn't hurt things any, to say the least. It wouldn't do any harm to join the two places together, giving it more meaning.

Carl's parents were farmers in the Shenston area, and he was to be the last baby born to his father, Robert, and his mother, Beatrice Andrews Bolen. Thus, being the last baby born probably meant he got away with lots of stuff his older siblings didn't. Parents with large families seemed to slack off on the rules after a bit. Maybe they just can't keep track of the shenanigans anymore, or else they could just be plain worn out from all the years of parenting. From the stories Carl told me, he was treated with respect and I'm thinking this was one of the reasons he grew up to be the kind, gentle man he was.

He was given responsibilities not usually given to young boys, and he enjoyed his life growing up on the family farm. This has got to be the reason for his sunny, quiet nature, I'm sure. He was showered with love. In later years, he was referred to as one of those *Bolen Boys*: there were eight boys and four girls in his family. My family were also farmers North of Stratton in the Pattullo district and had eight girls and four boys, an equal number of children, only the opposite. I was known and referred to as one of those *Schram Girls*.

Who would have thought? Did that mean the stars were lined up back then? Who knows? Anyway, it ended up pretty good if I do say so myself, and like the song says: "We believe in Happy Endings." Yes, we were happy through the years, right up until the end, with Carl still smiling.

As a young boy, Carl was fortunate to have his grandpa living with his family. His grandpa got to know his little grandson, Carl, quite well, following him around, helping to keep him from getting into trouble. This chore kept his grandpa busy, for Carl never slowed down, on the go steady. He could hear his grandpa's voice as he followed him around. "Charlie," (that's what he called him—it had a nicer ring to it), "Charlie, what are you doing now?" "Where are you going now, Charlie?"

Grandpa gave his mother a much-needed break, I'm sure. Carl's sister, Kay, told me that Carl used to jump in his mother's bed at six o'clock in the morning with a story book and want her to read it to him. She thought that he had something wrong back then and threatened to take him to the doctor if this kept up. He should still be in bed sleeping like normal kids, not up and raring to go at this early hour, she felt. More than likely, he had a passion for life and enjoyed being busy. By staying in bed, he might miss out on something important in his daily adventures.

On one of their outings, Carl's grandpa saved Carl's life. If it weren't for grandpa, Carl wouldn't have had the life journey he did. On the family farm, they had a creek running behind their farmhouse—every young boy's dream, if I can imagine it. Think of the fun trying to catch frogs and other water creatures! It could prove to be a dangerous place to play for a young boy, though, and it must have kept grandpa a little on edge, to say the least. At the creek, Carl stepped out onto a big green rock—or so he thought—ending up under the water. It wasn't a rock at all, but some of that green stuff that tends to grow on the water—algae or something of that nature, I think. Grandpa fished him out and gave him a scolding. Carl's little brown boots were full of water, and I'm thinking his grandpa probably pulled him out by his suspenders as he used to wear them back in the day, trying to copy his older brothers, more than likely.

Being small for his age could possibly have been another reason for the suspenders. That way he didn't have the worry of his pants falling down off his narrow hips. He was always small for his age. In fact, his sister, Kay, had once told me that when he was sixteen years old, he wore size ten clothes. Buying clothes for a young man who wore kid's sizes meant a trip to the children's store to see what they had to offer in the line of big boy attire. One had to choose carefully, I'm sure— something to make him look more his age than his size suggested.

Size didn't matter when it came to helping out on the family farm, though. To enable him to drive the tractor, he perched on a wooden milk crate with wooden blocks on the pedals so his feet could reach and he could control his driving. With his cap perched safely on his head, he was off to the races, a happy camper. Like I've always said, there's more than one way to skin a cat (as the old saying from back in the day goes, which brings another picture to mind, not a pleasant one, especially for animal lovers). I don't think this method of driving the tractor would pass a safety inspection with today's standards, but it did the trick and everything worked out well, and Carl was able to get in a good day's work.

I can't forget to mention another little chore Carl enjoyed which also made him feel proud. This was sitting next to his mother when she was knitting, holding the ball of yarn, keeping it from getting tangled. He enjoyed this closeness with his mom, being her little helper. From carefully watching her, he learned how to knit also. And if she was called away to attend to another matter, he would take up the knitting where she had left off. To picture this is worth more than a thousand words, one I'd love to see. He may have been small, but he certainly proved he could do anything he set his mind to.

In his early years, too young to have a driver's license, he chauffeured his older siblings around and about to their special events. He had to sit on cushions in the car to enable him to see over the dash and out the windshield at the road ahead—a good safety measure. Once, when he was passenger with his siblings in the car (he couldn't remember who was doing the driving on that occasion) they had the misfortune of upsetting the car over onto its top. Not a pretty sight with his siblings frantically scrambling to get out to safety!

In the middle of this melee, he lost his cap and couldn't find it. Even into his later years he couldn't figure out why he was so upset about losing his cap, for they never did make one to fit his head. It was more likely that they were upside down that upset him the most, being a top-notch driver himself. Caps all tended to be too big for Carl and liked to rest on his ears. In all our married years, we were never fortunate enough to find one that fit properly and that didn't need some adjustments. Sometimes a paper clip, or a piece of cardboard inserted, would tighten up the fit enough to do justice to the cap perched on his head.

After this losing-his-cap incident and being upside down on the road, when things settled down and the dust cleared, the result was Carl becoming the chauffeur. From now on, he would be the main driver. In fact, he had the honour of driving the ladies home from the Lutheran Ladies Institute meetings. This was a prestigious job at this young age. Oftentimes they had their gatherings at his home, working on their quilting and such, and would require a ride home after. They would pay him a quarter for this service, which he probably spent on peppermints, a treat he was fond of.

At this time in his life he now had a dog, which was black and white and named Mickey. Mickey also had a liking for his young master's peppermints. They were soulmates, belonging together. When Carl had hidden a bag of peppermints under his bed tied to the bed springs, Mickey found them and polished them off. Just the brown paper bag, looking dejected and empty, was all that was left of this treat that he had thought was in a safe enough place for future enjoyment. Carl had saved his own money to buy Mickey, so he found this incident to be a bit of an unexpected disappointment from his pet.

Now this Mickey dog seemed to have his problems as well. Maybe back then he had Alzheimer's like his master later in life. Mickey's memory didn't seem to be all that good or else there was the possibility that he just liked dancing to his own tune, like Carl and me. Anyway, this "chasing cars" that he enjoyed doing so much wasn't working out to be the safest for him, and it was sure to be his hang-up.

Carl had a love of cars, so maybe God had a hand in this, bringing these soulmates together. After one particularly exhilarating chase, Mickey came home with an eye missing. Then on another, the result was a leg going in the wrong direction. He finally lost a leg, which didn't seem to slow him down any. When Carl told me of the misfortunes his pet suffered, I asked him, "How did Mickey deal with these setbacks?" He told me Mickey would lie around for a few days and then he was good to go again. See what I mean? These farm boy's pets were just living their dream as well, having their fun wherever they found it, or in lots of cases, making their own. (Not all of it behind the proverbial barn, as the song goes.)

The two of them, Carl and Mickey, made a good pair: they enjoyed life, they were both energetic, and they tried to prove themselves by doing a good job. Whether it was chasing cars in Mickey's case, or in Carl's case in later years, working hard in the bush. His wood pile was always a bit higher than the piles of any of the other men he worked with. He enjoyed seeing the bonus on his paycheque for the extra effort he put into the job. Makes me wonder if Carl's goal was to prove himself to be a man and not a boy as his size depicted.

Mickey's injuries came from chasing cars, whereas Carl's came later in life from his hard work making a living doing what he liked best. Carl loved working in the forest with the smell of pine trees and breathing in the fresh air with the feel of the sunshine on his face. The animals that he encountered, the beauty of the wildflowers, all this made a perfect setting for the perfect job.

Carl and Mickey made a good pair, having lots in common like their love of peppermints, their energy, and their drive for life in general or for the chase, as you might want to call it. They were meant for each other, soulmates, a boy and his dog: neither of them giving up easily.

From pictures Carl has of his pet, I'm sure he was a sheep dog, black and white in colour, and his ability to run like the wind makes me think I could be correct. Can you visualize the picture? The poor sheep wouldn't have stood a fair chance in this race, if it ever came to pass. The outcome wouldn't have been one of victory for the sheep. Mickey, with his black and white hair blowing in the wind, lost in the throes of his passion to chase… The sheep running at top speed, wondering what was happening, balls of wool flying in all directions… Lord! What a picture this makes! You could probably gather enough wool to knit a good sweater and still have yarn left over to darn a few pairs of socks.

Carl

Carl, his mom and Mickey "her little helper."

Carl, Mickey and the farm house... Note the depth of the snow.

Carl trying out his luck on stilts.

Carl on tricycle with Kay's doll.

Carl living dangerously perched on the rain barrel, blowing a whistle.

Carl, (I would say some iodine was used here), still smiling.

Carl living dangerously perched on the rain barrel, blowing a whistle.

Carl, (I would say some iodine was used here), still smiling.

Carl trying out his luck on stilts.

Carl on tricycle with Kay's doll.

CHAPTER TWO

The Learning Years

How Carl came to getting Mickey is another story, one which I agree is difficult to comprehend but nevertheless is true. Mickey had a price tag on him for some strange reason. I find it unbelievable that a boy would have to pay for a dog in the first place. Maybe he was a special breed like I thought. His older brothers gave Carl a hand by setting him up with a project to raise the cash. It was a venture that paid more than the twenty-five cents he received for chauffeuring the Lutheran ladies, which he was more than happy to get at the time.

This new adventure was to take place under the cover of night with only the moonlight for guidance. His brothers supplied him with bottles of wine to sell at the local dances at the schoolhouse, which was on his family's property, I believe. He hid the wine in the grass alongside the fence and also in the church across the road from the school. He charged one dollar a bottle for this fine beverage. If you cared to have more fun and wanted to enjoy a good dance, you had to make it worthwhile. And alcohol was known, back in the day, to give you more courage if you were a bit shy around the girls. Your personality was sure to change, like night and day. And who in their right mind wants to sit on the bench all night instead of having fun dancing with the girls, especially if you were sweet on one of them.

Carl, being a young lad, never tried this wine, so he wasn't personally aware of the consequences of drinking it—other than knowing if you sampled it, fun was sure to be had. Back in the day they called it "porch

15

climber." And, as the name implies, it could be quite a powerful drink and the results could be endless—other than just having fun on the dance floor.

Selling wine proved to be quite profitable, to say the least, and hiding the bottles in the church was a sign that the Lord had a hand in Carl's profits. The Lord knew Mickey was going to need a special boy to care for him, one who would be understanding and help him with this running addiction of his, and not pass judgment on his shortcomings. The fact that Carl attended church on Sundays with his mom, dressed up in his white shirt and looking angelic in his Sunday best, was sure to have been a good thing. God knew him personally, I'm certain of that.

Life is good when you're young and having fun, just the way it should be. It's like that old saying, "more fun than a barrel of monkeys." Thinking back on it now, Carl and Mickey were a couple of hardworking monkeys...that just wouldn't give up. They didn't need wine. They just danced to their own tune and had fun doing it.

There had to be issues with Carl's thinking cap back then, though. Was Alzheimer's lurking in the background, waiting to make an appearance? Maybe it was waiting in the shadows letting him enjoy a few good years before putting on the brakes, so to speak. Who knows? It sure makes me wonder. Was my special man earmarked at an early age for this journey?

There was one occasion when Carl did something that ended up on his list of things you shouldn't do… He dug a deep hole in the snow at the fence where his family crossed. To get to the school, you had to cross the fence here as well. After digging this hole, he made it into a snow trap, covering the opening with branches and more snow. He went off home feeling quite proud of this, I'm sure. It was quite clever, he thought—smarter than Mickey chasing cars.

Now then, Carl's father was Irish with the red hair that goes with this honour. Carl could still remember how red his face was that night, brighter than his hair when he came into the house. And it didn't take long to figure out that he was madder than a wet hen! Of course, he was the one who fell into the snow trap on the way home from a hard day working in the bush. A taste of his Irish temper was on the menu that night, you can bet. This was one of the lessons Carl learned on his way to growing up and one he wouldn't repeat. He learned to think things over before someone was injured. He felt bad that he had caused his dad this stress after working hard in the snow all day. His dad was always a kind and gentle man.

Thinking back, Carl didn't fare too badly. He had the job of carrying in the stove wood at the schoolhouse, stacking it up and keeping it neat and tidy. In the morning, he would go back and light the stove so it would be cozy for the teacher when she arrived. May as well start the day off by keeping the teacher happy! Nothing wrong with that... Another chore on his list was to bring in a fresh pail of cold water for the students, hanging the ladle on the bucket for them. Yes, from all of his special memories, he was a pretty good boy and thrived on responsibilities at an early age.

Returning to the colour red as mentioned earlier, this colour signified trouble when it had something to do with his father's face, and it also signified trouble for Carl at a later time. Some of the older men who gathered at the Stratton Hotel on a regular basis were always busy thinking of pranks to play on unsuspecting people. They decided to play one on an older gentleman with whom they had the occasional beer. They knew this gentleman would get worked up over this, and they could barely contain themselves with this idea of theirs. Maybe they had drunk one too many pints or didn't think things through well enough, but the plan was to paint the old fellow's prized pig red.

They bought the red paint and hired Carl, of course, to do the job on Halloween night after dark. So, Carl climbed into the pen and, with all of his artistic abilities, painted the pig—doing a fine job. In the meantime, the old fellow wasn't home. More than likely he was at the parlour having a few bedtime sips before turning in for the night. It was all done in fun, but it didn't turn out that way and didn't end up as planned. The pig didn't survive the painting job. I had heard it has something to do with pores covered in paint and the pig not surviving because of this.

Carl felt very sad after this incident, which was all done in fun. And I can just imagine how the adults who hired him felt. There was surely a lesson to be learned there, I'm thinking. They say you learn by doing. Carl was certainly proving this to be true, in a few cases anyway. Having fun could have its drawbacks for sure and could take that beautiful smile off his face for a while.

It was at an early age when he decided it was high time to get an important piece of paper for his wallet. He set off to Rainy River in pursuit of a driver's license, driving himself there, a distance of at least 20 to 30 miles on a gravel road. This would bring him much pride and joy in the years to come along with his love of cars—this would be the much-needed proof that he was a qualified driver. Fibbing about his age to the license issuer, he was asked how many miles he thought he had driven. After Carl gave him a good figure, the man said, "You must know how to drive then," and wrote him out a license.

One can only imagine the ride back home to Shenston, the excitement of having a valid driver's license in his possession. Wow! The magic of it all! This growing up was just the greatest, like being on top of the world. There was no looking back now. Life was certainly moving forward for this young man. I can just imagine how proud his father and mother were of their boy who was on the way to being a man.

Growing up, Carl spent more of his time with two siblings in particular: his brother Frankie and sister Kay. They were close to him in age, which probably explains this. His brother William, the oldest of the children, was twenty when Carl was born, so I would imagine he was already out on his own by then. Kay was like his twin; they both had the same health issues and had the same surgery with the same doctor. And both were in the hospital together at a later date.

Carl enjoyed teasing his older brothers and being a pest, like little boys tend to be at times. Once, after annoying them while they were playing cards, Frankie decided to settle him down by hanging him on a nail out in the barn so they could enjoy some peace and quiet. I can almost imagine the racket coming from the barn that day. He probably raised the rafters with all the noise he made! The startled barn swallows must have flown off looking for a place to hide, worried about their nests and if they were going to survive this commotion or not. Even Mickey likely went and hid in a safe spot with his paws over his ears, worrying about the safety of the boy who was raising such a ruckus and wondering if there was anything he could do to help his young master.

Yes, this was life on the farm. Made you wonder how you survived sometimes!

After this incident, the two boys remained good friends and Frankie would often ask for Carl's help if he needed a second pair of hands. This made Carl proud. Like the day Frankie was putting in fence posts, for instance, and asked for help. Carl got to hold the posts straight while his big brother drove them into the ground with the sledgehammer. This proved to be all fun and games and big boy stuff. That is, until the sledgehammer head came off the handle from the force of being brought down on the post and went flying, hitting Carl directly in the stomach! When he came back to life—or in other words, when the lights came back on—he was lying on his back with the toes of his little brown boots pointing towards the sky.

Lord! I guess the pain was the worst he had ever felt. That's how severe it was! And it's lucky for him that it didn't strike him in the head. I don't think that would have helped his situation in the future, given what he would later face. If he would have survived, that is. He was to be in enough trouble as it was.

Later on, Carl did his own version of seeing what further damage he could do to his belly that Frankie hadn't already done. This took place when he was pushing a wheelbarrow quite fast and hit a speed bump, of sorts, which brought him to a sudden stop. Once again, he was on his back looking up at the clouds, trying really hard to breathe through all the pain.

This growing up thing was proving to be hard on his belly, as well as wearing on his nerves, what with all the pain and everything. Living and growing up on the farm as a child was reason enough for creating your own fun—be it painful or not. You just took a chance if something crossed your mind and hoped you got some enjoyment out of it without breaking your neck or something equally as serious. Farm moms usually had clean cloths on hand that they would tear into strips and use to bandage you up if there was a sign of bleeding. They also kept a bottle of iodine in the medicine cabinet to disinfect a cut. The sting of this was punishment enough for hurting yourself and was sure to make you squeal.

To top it all off, in the midst of all these mishaps, Carl may have been causing more problems with his brain than he realized. The hard landings and the lights going out couldn't have been a good thing. It could make a person wonder, seeing what the future had in store.

I wonder where Grandpa was at the time when all this injury and pain was going down. Maybe he was having a much-needed nap, getting a bit worn out trying to keep up to this active young lad. I can imagine he worried about Carl making it through his boyhood days still in one piece with all his body parts intact. Gosh, it probably made him tired just thinking about the seriousness of it all. A good snooze was surely in order. Grandpas tend to worry more as they get older. They aren't quite as fast on their feet anymore, and this could create a problem.

———⁓⁓◦◦◦◦◦⁓⁓———

Those *Bolen Boys*, they were a force to contend with, that's for sure—when they were in their growing up stages, especially. They knew how to have fun too, or better yet, make their own fun on a Saturday night. Not that they were looking for trouble, or anything like that. No, they didn't have a mean bone in their bodies that I knew of. But sometimes you know how trouble seems to find you...when you're not looking for it. Like I said before, they often had one too many. That "Old V" could put you in a different place at times.

This kept you wanting more of this level of excitement, wondering what else might be in store to cap off the good old Black Hawk dances. For a few of the boys who participated in the fun, that usually took place on the dance floor. Crawling out of bed on a Sunday morning meant a quick check for black eyes, making sure the swelling of the nose wasn't too noticeable after a bit of blood loss, and making sure the nose was still lined up in a normal fashion and not broken. Some tested their bruised bodies, seeing if they still hurt as much as they remembered from their recollections of the night before and the activities they had taken part in.

After this it was a trip down the stairs for a good cup of strong coffee to get them back on their feet again, ready to start a new day. Black Hawk was the place to be on a Saturday night! If you didn't show

up sometime during the evening you just weren't living right, trust me! Everyone in their right mind worked this into their schedule on a Saturday night, not wanting to miss out on any of the excitement that was sure to take place. These encounters on a Saturday night at the Black Hawk dances were date nights for farm girls and boys for sure. Nobody got hurt too bad that a little bit of time didn't heal till you were good as new again. Nobody got arrested, though some came close and squeaked by, from my recollections.

Gosh, the memories! Something to enjoy as you sit back and proceed to grow old. They are precious and dear to a person's heart. You can re-live your life over and over and maybe change it if you want—whatever suits you best. The dances themselves were just what the country folk enjoyed—their kind of music for sure. A live country band, singing and performing on the stage...and watching the antics on the dance floor! It sort of reminded me of the movie *Road House,* but a lot tamer. Just a certain amount of animosity between some of the boys which caused a lot of wrestling matches.

Black Hawk also served Sloppy-Joes to the hungry dancers. They were the greatest, or so we thought. To this day I still remember them. Later in life, I called the lady who made them and got her recipe so I could serve them at our stock car races in Atikokan. One never forgets the good things in life that you once enjoyed.

I recall one particular Saturday night when Carl and I got a ride to the dance with a fellow from Stratton who was home from California for a vacation of sorts. He was driving a big fancy convertible; impressive to say the least, like he may have found the gold they sing about in that song. You know the one: "All the Gold in California." Also, I must mention that he had a bottle of gin that he was sipping from. Not a good pastime, drinking and driving—unsafe to say the least. A bit unsettling for me! As we neared the hall, we noticed the police standing outside illuminated in the car's head lights.

The next scary thing for me was that this man in question tucked the bottle into my new straw purse which was open on the top. So much for fashion, but the bottle fit perfectly and was not noticeable. The police sprang into action when we pulled up, opening our car doors. They allowed Carl and I to go into the hall, and I still don't know what happened to our driver. Apparently, the big limousine that he was driving belonged to somebody in California and had been reported stolen. I guess this adds some truth to that song, "All the Gold in California," which goes like this: "*...is in a bank in the middle of Beverly Hills in somebody else's name.*" It didn't matter where he'd played before (Stratton), California is a brand-new game. Yes, the story of one country boy trying to make it look like he had hit it big. He was sure to impress the unsuspecting farm girls...until he got caught! Darn the luck, anyway!

A few years later, Carl heard the man was in jail in Winnipeg for forgery. This was a sure sign of not giving up easily. He was quite a nice-looking man, but he was building up the wrong reputation for sure, getting the wrong kind of attention, the kind you should stay away from. Hopefully he would soon run out of bricks and mend his ways, take a different path down that gravel road, travel a bit slower, take time to think before hitting the highway. There is always a chance one can change given the right incentive.

This story sort of brings to mind that Mickey dog who didn't give up easily. Losing an eye and a leg didn't stop him from showing off his running ability which he used to impress his master, show him what he was good at. That's the only way to plan your moves.

———〜∽◦◦◦✕◦◦◦∽〜———

Carl had a good buddy and soulmate who he worked with in the bush and also had fun just "hanging out" with, having growing up adventures together. His name was Garfield Faragher and they still remained good friends until the last, still laughing together when sharing their memories of the fun times. They learned a lot about life and just maybe a little bit about love on their journey and enjoyed every minute of it. Everyone should be so lucky as to have a good friend like Garfield. They spent their early years working together in the bush and ended up at Mando where they stayed in the notorious "bunkhouses" north of Atikokan.

They worked hard in the bush and just as hard trying to plot a way to get back down to the country for some weekend fun. At this time, there was no highway between Atikokan and Fort Frances. This was to cause hardship for the young men. And, from what I read in Carl's letters from the bunkhouse, it resulted in lots of loneliness in not being able to get to visit with their loved ones as often as they wished. Riding in the empty boxcars was not always a good solution—they had to try to keep warm, and also try to avoid getting caught by the CNR policemen, which happened on occasion.

Garfield enjoyed making an appearance at the Black Hawk dances as well. Nobody wanted to miss out on these adventures, that's for sure. He was someone you had to keep an eye on...in case he needed help settling someone down. Making sure he didn't lose a shoe or something, which happened now and then. There was a certain few who came to the dances just looking for a scrap, wanting to be cock of the roost, show off a bit.

He was good at keeping everyone on a level playing field, taking the bull out of the steer and keeping the overzealous boys settled down. The boys used this as a ruse for impressing the farm girls who stood on the sidelines watching their antics. There were quite a few Saturday nights when there wasn't too much dancing going on, more wrestling than anything. Sort of like watching *Wrestlemania* you can see on TV these days. Getting back to all this and wondering, maybe it was something in the water. Or else, maybe it was something they were mixing the water with.

Back in the day, Garfield continued to be an idol for some, a force to be reckoned with. He was most likely the handsomest young man of the bunch; and in my opinion, Carl was the other one. They were the opposite in terms of looks, with Garfield having sparkling dark eyes and dark hair and Carl having blue eyes and blond curls dangling on his forehead. But they both had the same beautiful smiles. It's no wonder they made such good friends. Their friendship lasted even until they were both grandpas. And to top it off, they were both still looking good.

Saturday nights left the blood pumping in your veins from sheer excitement. If you didn't have fun on a Saturday night, you just weren't living right! After the dance, we'd gather at the Bolen's home, and then midnight hunger would be a force to reckon with. By then the Sloppy-Joes had worn off and the growing boys were hungry for a bedtime snack. With much fun and giggles, this meant a trip to a neighbouring chicken coop for a couple of fat hens…before they got caught by a barking dog that would surely waken the farmer. Not an adventure for farm boys to be proud of, being with all the hard work that took place trying to get ahead and live off the land. Also, the loss of two eggs a day would be missed by the farm wife and it saddens me to think of it now.

Arriving home after this chicken robbing escapade, with country tunes blasting and feathers flying, fresh chicken was on the menu that night as well as on a few other nights that I can recall. You couldn't wish for anything fresher than that! And you probably never got to enjoy it again in the years following the closure of the Black Hawk doors. If you never took the plunge, you missed out on a lot of good living. Good farm kind of fun, that is for sure. These special memories will stay with you forever.

After the feast of fresh chicken and of course the ride home, the next challenge was to try and sneak into the house without waking anyone—namely parents! They didn't seem to care much for the fact that their daughters were arriving home just before sun-up on a Sunday morning. Oh well…we survived the consequences—the tongue lashing that is—secretly thinking it was all worth it.

After managing to get a few hours of solid sleep, it was time to rise and shine and start a new day. Our morning chores were now awaiting our attention. By the next morning, thoughts about the agenda for the next Saturday night were already on our mind, as well as feeding the chickens and milking the cows. Hopefully some more of that good old-fashioned fun, something to keep your blood pressure up, make you come alive again. Seeing the boys on the dance floor would surely do that to a person.

Kay, Carl, Frankie, three youngest Bolen children.

Carl, the chauffeur on the left, Frankie second from the right.

Family Car – Carl's first driving experience.

CHAPTER THREE

Love and Loss

After seeing a few live hockey games in later years, I'm quite sure Carl would have made a top-notch player if given the chance. The way he handled his game back then, the way he played it out…he could have gone places. He enjoyed the planning ahead, making shots when the coast was clear, taking an odd penalty here and there along the way, trying to score a goal…maybe all he needed was a good pair of skates. This may have helped him with his game plan.

He enjoyed living his life in a happy-go-lucky kind of way, always putting his best shot forward. Some of his living was a little faster than what the speed limit allowed. But then it wasn't set very high back then. The lawmen seemed to be quite a bit stricter if you were caught doing something you shouldn't be doing. That's where the penalties came into play.

Before I forget, I'm going to stop and apologize for this fast driving and fast living right now! All this disregard for danger was not a good thing! So sorry, God, but it was all in fun. Hopefully you won't be too discouraged with Carl's actions and it won't cause a problem at the "Big Gate." What boy wouldn't want to enjoy his life if he's given a fair chance to have a bit of fun?

I would be remiss if I didn't mention the few extra miles Carl enjoyed putting on his "car of the day" back then. This little thing called love (I think, now that I'm up on things) was all part of his game plan after we kicked up our heels in our favourite place. It was such a nice way of unwinding after the evening fun was all over. Driving down those proverbial back country roads on a Saturday night with our favourite country tunes softly playing—it was a perfect ending for a perfect day. Saturday was the only night to take on this adventure for sure, a good way of topping off the week before beginning a new one. With the night sky above and the glow from the stars lighting up the way ahead, romance was in the air. Sometimes we would startle an unsuspecting deer enjoying a late-night snack along the road. A pretty sight, with their big eyes peering at you in the darkness. As if they are wondering, *Hey! What's going on here?*

Most times Carl would park the car and we would just sit quietly, taking in this vision of nature's beauty. Our young hearts would beat a tune of their own…just the two of us…enjoying ourselves! Being glad to be alive and in love on a Saturday night. Some nights we would be rudely interrupted in our time of quietness and peace. The magic of the night would be broken by the appearance of headlights coming at us in the distance—a sure sign it was time to move along. Yes, that special moment in time was over for now, until the next weekend you hoped, when you would do it all over again.

———— ∿⦿⦿⦿⦿⦿∿ ————

From his days living in Shenston as a boy, Carl had other close friends. The McKenzie family lived down the road from Carl's family. If I remember right, there were four girls in the family and two boys. One of the daughters, Leone, still lives in Stratton, and we were fortunate to meet her now and again on our trips to Stratton. In earlier years, her husband found work in Atikokan and boarded with us when we were newlyweds living in a small house on McKenzie Avenue. The house had actually been brought into town after the Mando camps had closed, and we were fortunate enough to be able to rent it. There was a huge shortage of housing with the town starting to boom, and we ended up with five boarders at our home, all of them needing hot meals, lunches, laundry and for some of them, a place to sleep.

I may have only been around twenty years old, but they were happy with my cooking. I would get up at six o'clock in the morning to start my day, baking fresh pies, cooking breakfast for hungry men, and getting them off to work. Later on, I heard there were favourable complements about my cooking going around Stratton, a good pat on the back for sure. Lord! It was a lot of work for a young girl who was new at this playing house stuff. Keeping a bunch of men happily fed and clothed. I still don't know how I managed to keep going. I must have been hyper-active or something of that nature. Of course, Carl would have helped with the dishes. That, I'm quite sure of!

I don't think that I could do that sort of thing today. If someone wanted something special in their lunch, they could possibly end up making their own, the way I feel now! I guess I was too hard on my body in my younger days what with all the strenuous work I put in on the farm and working at a tourist camp in Nestor Falls (daylight till dark). Not to mention the sleep I lost on those Saturday nights that I told you about earlier. That couldn't have helped the situation any.

One thing I did learn back then was if you didn't get your needed sleep, it was lost forever. You would never get it back and it would surely haunt you when your alarm clock kicked in at five or six o'clock in the morning. I will be the first to admit that I still didn't learn my lesson, though. This growing up could be just as hard on the young girls, taking a toll on their bodies, almost as much as it was on the boys who enjoyed wrestling on the dance floor.

Taking in boarders was a good lesson in pushing me to the limit. But again, all the men were from Stratton, and you just couldn't say no to your fellow teammates when they were in need. This came from being raised on a farm in a close-knit community where neighbours helped neighbours. Some of the farming activities were just too much for one person, especially with the short seasons when haying and harvesting almost caused a panic. It could mean the loss of a crop, hard work, and of course, financial harm if it weren't for neighbours helping each other out in their time of need.

As I mentioned, the McKenzie family were good family friends of the Bolen's and lived a short way down the road from them. Carl enjoyed playing with the girls, Leone and Bessie, while he was still a boy and spent lots of time at their house. Once when Carl's mom was in Thunder Bay, she sent Carl a small pack of snapshot views from Port

Arthur, dated 1946. She included a note with the pictures of famous places that read as follows:

To Carl from Mom: *"How are you? Tough as ever I suppose. Do you still visit the McKenzie's? Grandpa was asking about you."*

This short note put a smile on my face when I read it. The mention of him being tough as ever sounded just like the young man I grew to love. Being tough as ever sounds like he never gave up, even as a young boy. And he certainly hadn't changed over the years. The mention of Grandpa asking about him meant that Carl's grandpa was also in Thunder Bay, hopefully just visiting and not for medical purposes, and still worrying about his young grandson. Carl would be eight years old at this time, and he already had the McKenzie family for his friends, walking down the road to visit them.

It's strange how a short note can draw a picture in your mind of what life must have been like some seventy years ago. A young, blond-haired boy, wearing suspenders to hold up his britches, fearlessly walking down the gravel road kicking stones with his little brown boots, going to visit his friends. His black and white dog Mickey was probably trotting along beside him, happy to be with him on this beautiful sunny day. Yes, it's great just thinking now that this boy was already earmarked to be my future husband.

Carl had an older brother, Clarence, born on November 13, 1921. His friends, the McKenzie family, had a son also named Clarence. Clarence McKenzie was born on June 11, 1921. These two Clarence boys were soulmates, growing up together in the country. They ran the roads together having fun, enjoying their lives as boys tend to do.

It was war time and the two buddies enlisted to help our country in its time of need. Canada's young men were enlisting to help gain our freedom and put an end to this God-forsaken battle. Too many moms were left waiting at home for sons who wouldn't be returning, who bravely gave up their lives for their country, their homeland. Six months after enlisting, Carl's brother was posted for duty in the Normandy area in July, 1944. His buddy, Clarence McKenzie, was also posted for duty there.

Even though he was only six years old at the time, Carl could still remember the night the knock on the door came. A man who he remembered as being a Mr. Wilson from the telegraph office was standing at the door and gave them the message. Their son and brother was missing in action...and presumed dead. Carl said you could have heard a pin drop. Silence...

Clarence was only twenty-two years old. Still no more than a boy, he was young, handsome with a lot of good life left to live. Carl thought that he and Clarence looked a lot alike: same blond curly hair, same sparkling blue eyes, same beautiful smile, and of course, the same zest for life. Always the drive—the need to do your best! No matter what was thrown at you.

This news was heart wrenching. To lose your life so early, just as it was beginning. Carl still remembered his father getting up, grabbing the milk bucket, and heading out to the barn to milk the cow. That's what he did to handle his sorrow. As he left the house, he said: "It's a God damn world!"

At this time his dad was sixty-two years old and this devastating news added years to his face. There was lots of pain and silence in the house that night, something Carl would always remember. The shock, the disbelief! His brother who had enjoyed his life on the farm with his family, growing up to be a carefree young man, wouldn't be coming home. Ever!!

I remember the evening Carl told me the story of the two Clarences. I could hear both the pain and pride in his voice as he spoke: pain from the loss of his brother, and pride he had sacrificed his life for his country.

Carl's family received word that Clarence's body had been recovered, and he had been buried with honour in the *Bretteville-Sur-Laize Canadian War Cemetery* in Calvados, France. Later on, the family received a letter from a soldier who was with him that fateful night. He had written that he had stayed with Clarence, offering him comfort until the end. He also said that he didn't suffer. Lord, the sadness of it all! Men fighting to save their country together as friends! Dying in each other's arms...

The letter from the stranger brought with it some comfort and peace, knowing that their boy didn't suffer alone on that fateful night. It also raised their spirits knowing that the stranger had taken the time to set their minds at ease and lessen some of the pain of their loss.

Carl promised to be a good soldier for his brother, doing what he had to do, marching on every day. Clarence would be proud of him, just like Carl was proud of his big brother.

In 1944, the McKenzie family also received a telegram saying their son was missing in action. About two months later they received a second telegram now stating that he was killed in action. Both families were now suffering the painful loss of their two boys.

The McKenzie family later received a third telegram stating that their son had actually been captured and was a prisoner of war. Finally, they received a letter from Clarence himself saying that he was wounded, hit in the leg by a piece of shrapnel. He was being looked after by a French nurse, but all he could have was black bread and water.

When the war ended in 1945, he was sent to England where his leg had to be amputated. After getting back home to Stratton, he was fitted with a wooden leg a few months later. His father, Ken, also had a wooden leg, having been injured in an accident while working in the bush.

Clarence McKenzie lost his life in August 1956 in a tragic motor vehicle accident while on his way to work. He had the misfortune of going over the Pinewood Bridge (a Bailey Bridge) in his car, and drowning. The bridge was narrow and not the best, I was told. He is buried in the Stratton Cemetery. Yes, it's like Mr. Bolen said, "It's a God Damn World!"

Alice McKenzie, Clarence's mom, belonged to the Shenston Women's Institute, so she most likely benefitted from a few rides home from the meetings at the Bolen home with Carl being the chauffeur, thus helping him to purchase the peppermints that he enjoyed.

Carl had a second elder brother, Donald, born March 5,1919. He was also posted for duty in the Canadian Army and did so for the next three and a half years with part of his time spent serving in Jamaica. While home on leave, he married his sweetheart, Stella Watts. Their war experience ended on a happier note with them beginning their married life in the Shenston area. They were blessed with two sons, Donald Melvin and Jack Allen.

The Bolen family had already lost three of their children prior to the tragedy of losing Clarence. They had lost twin baby girls in 1920,

the year before Clarence was born. Then in 1934, another son, Norman, passed away after being stricken with meningitis at the age of four. Carl's mom had said that Norman was showing signs of improvement, but then later when she went upstairs to check on him, he had passed away. The angels had come for him.

Such a terrible loss of loved ones! More than enough pain for one family to bear! Maybe this is why they raised their children in their carefree way, letting them make their own decisions and their own life choices, treating them with respect. Letting them make their own mistakes on their journeys through the early years, when your choices were important, and loving them through it all. Yes, we need to let our babies have fun. Life can be too short. Let them enjoy themselves for however long it may be.

Clarence Bolen
Nov 18 1921 – Aug 04 1944

Clarence McKenzie
June 11, 1921 – Aug 1956

Clarence R Bolen
Military Headstone

Rows of Canadian Military Headstones in a Graveyard in France.

The Two Clarences

Two Friends
 Two Close Neighbours
  Enlisted in the military together

Clarence Bolen, born November 13, 1921. Died in action on August 4, 1944.

Clarence McKenzie, born June 11, 1921. Wounded in action. Taken prisoner. After the war ended in 1945, he was sent to England where he had his leg amputated. Later, after returning home to Stratton, he was fitted with a wooden leg. He later passed away in a tragic motor vehicle accident on the Pinewood bridge in August 1956.

God Bless these two young friends who went off to war together. They faced the realities of battle. One came home injured; one remained behind.

Rest in Peace

CHAPTER FOUR

Man Things

A need for some serious cash and a love of cars had Carl's wheels turning, wondering how he could solve this problem. In 1952, at the age of fifteen, he left the family farm for the first time with another friend from Stratton, Donnie Penney. And together they headed east to Atikokan where all the action was taking place with the discovery of iron ore, thus beginning a period of mining fever. To travel, the two boys hopped on a freight train and rode the rails as there was no highway connecting Fort Frances and Atikokan; the CNR train was the only option for transportation. If you had no fear, you hopped on when the time was right, and it took you to your destination.

This was to be a good way for the men to travel, other than driving for hours, going through the States to the Pigeon River Crossing and arriving in Atikokan. It also gave them some extra time to spend in the country with their girlfriends, if I remember correctly. Now, what young man wouldn't try this mode of travel, taking that proverbial chance of getting caught?

Carl was told once, after he was caught, that it could be either seven days or thirty days in jail. Why the difference? I have no idea. He was let off with a stern warning. A gentle stern warning, that is. I think the CNR policeman was being kind to them and understood their plight, having been young once himself and still remembering what love was all about back then. This journey didn't prove profitable for Carl who didn't end up getting a job out of it. Maybe, I'm thinking, his size could have had something to do with this. He returned home with plans to try again at a later date.

At the age of seventeen, Carl lost his mother. This was a great loss for the youngest boy of the family who was so attached to his mom and enjoyed all the time he had shared with her, not to mention all the help he gave her, being a good son. This blow also shattered his father's heart, one his father never recovered from. Carl drove her to the hospital that day and could still remember the way she kept looking at him, as if she didn't recognize him. He mentioned once that the cause of death was her heart. And he never spoke of this in future conversations. He never forgot her cooking and I tried my best to make him the same desserts he had enjoyed as a boy. I could tell that speaking of his mom was painful for Carl.

Carl later had the misfortune of losing yet another family member. His brother William, from Elliot Lake, Ontario, passed away from lung disease from years of working in the uranium mine. This happened just prior to Carl and I being married. I never had the opportunity to meet William. He was married and left behind a family who would face life without their father to guide them.

Lord, how much loss can one family endure? Carl took it upon himself to try to do as much as he could to help his father, knowing full well that his father's broken heart wasn't going to mend anytime soon. Nor were the tears he shed on a daily basis going to just up and stop. Yes, this loss of a special love, the mother of his babies, will do this to a man. Break his spirit. Take away the will to go on without her in his life.

Still only seventeen, two years after his first try, Carl decided to head back to Atikokan to see how his chances of finding a job would be this time. He was more determined than ever to find something. The time was right, after all that had happened, to take over the reins and be a young man with a paycheque. He got lucky and was hired by Steep Rock Iron Mines (CAC). Of course, this was after fibbing about his age and saying he was eighteen. He was getting to be quite good at this fibbing thing. It was starting to pay off for him.

His new job was dredging the mud off the bottom of Steep Rock Lake. Most of the lake had been drained and the iron ore was now sitting under the mud. Not the best job in the world if an accident was to happen and you were to fall into the mud. But being it was his first job and it involved getting a regular paycheque, that's all that was important at the time.

A young lad was willing to start anywhere with a yearning for a steady paycheque along with a love of cars. He was just eighteen years old when he bought his first car—a brand new 1956 Chevrolet, yellow and black in colour. With a price tag of $1,740.00, it would be a mere steal in today's market. On his first road trip home to the farm he was held up at the Pigeon River Border crossing for three hours. The guard on duty couldn't visualize an eighteen year old owning a brand-new car and thought that he had probably stolen it. Finally, after not being able to prove anything was amiss, they let him go on his merry way. He left, feeling a bit disappointed at how he was treated like a common criminal.

After this episode, his treatment when he was out driving was no different. He said he would get stopped every night and the boys in blue (also known as policemen) would ask to see his driver's licence. He said he almost wore it out taking it out of his wallet. Surely, they didn't have to see it this often! This behaviour nearly drove him to distraction. Not a respectable way to treat a nice young man with a flashy car. I don't know if they were trying to break his spirit or not, but it was high time they left him alone. He had a love for cars. Nothing wrong with that!

He was to later spend a good ten months locked up in the prison farm (a perfect rest from harassment and bullying so he could finally get some peace and quiet, I'm thinking). One of the boys in blue who enjoyed pulling him over on a nightly basis ended up wanting to purchase one of the cars Carl had been asked to take off the road. I'm still trying to figure this one out.

At the farm (where he worked off his ten-month sentence) he had a four-legged friend, a young calf that would follow him around all day. Funny that...treating him with the respect he deserved and being a good friend even if he had four legs and not two. At least this calf recognized the goodness in this young man.

The job at CAC Steep Rock removing the mud from the iron ore was to keep Carl busy for about three years before he moved on. The streets of Atikokan were red mud, not a nice thing to encounter after a rainstorm. It was a challenge trying to get the red iron ore stains out of the laundry on wash day. It tested many a house-wife's patience.

There was also a shortage of housing in these early years, with the mining excitement bringing in families looking for work. This caused a real crisis as the young men had no place to sleep, even though many homes were taking in boarders.

There was a large apartment building on West Main Street, known as the Landry Building, where you could grab a sleep for one dollar a night. When you got up, someone else was waiting to crawl into your bed for some much-needed rest. What a life! Frank, the owner of this building, had a jewellery store and repaired watches in a lower room. The knowledge that one can hang on to over the years!

I can also remember Frank helping my father build a new barn after our original one on the farm was ripped from its moorings in a violent windstorm. Frank was well known for his building sense and figuring out how to plan good, solid structures. One more thing I recall about Frank was how he enjoyed eating. I remember sitting around the kitchen table with him telling stories and of course, his huge belly laughs. Yes, we all enjoyed Frank and these missions of him volunteering his knowledge. Carl was fortunate enough to get some good night's rest at the Landry Building when he was in need, and he mentioned it throughout the years.

After leaving his "job in the mud," Carl went on to work at Mando, a pulp and paper company, until 1966. He worked in the bush, and at the beginning of this adventure, they used horses to pull up the logs before they were piled. In the earlier days they used Swede saws for cutting down the trees, eventually graduating to chain saws. It was a great invention and easier on the body: a much faster way to drop a tree. Later, trees were pulled out to the roadside with a skidder—another good invention.

When Carl was working in the area north of Atikokan, he stayed in one of the many bunkhouses provided by the Mando Company. This came complete with a single cot to sleep on. A cook was hired to feed the hungry workers in the dining room and to supply the men with packed lunches for their long day in the bush. The company also provided an airplane which handled those important letters that were painstakingly written to the girls back home who were waiting for news from their loved ones in the bush.

To this day, I still have all of those letters. I recently read them, once again, enjoying the old news and happenings from the bunkhouse. Of course, there wasn't much news when you're living in the wild away from civilization, but each one contained a weather report. Rain kept them in the bunkhouse and therefore much of the letter writing was done then. Once a week the company put on a movie for the men as recreational therapy, something to keep them in the bush and prevent cabin fever.

In one of his letters, Carl mentioned that Myrna Lori was supposed to come and sing and that he was happy to hear this news. His uncle, Les Andrews from Thunder Bay, had got her started in the music industry. She was a great singer, and one of her songs, "Are You Mine?" became famous. Carl's mother's family, the Andrews, were very gifted in the music industry, making some of their own instruments as well as being able to play anything and sing as well. The fiddle, accordion, and guitar were some of their favourites, if I remember correctly. What a great gift to be given for sure, one that gave them lots of enjoyment over the years.

Garfield was involved in this bunkhouse life as well, so between the two of them they tried to keep occupied when not working. In one letter, Carl wrote they were going to drive into town and take part in a game of bingo, hoping to win the jackpot which was quite high that evening. This was probably being held at the Moose Hall. It was a good way to spend some idle time and offered the hope of striking it rich in the meantime.

He bought himself a motorcycle for their enjoyment after working hard all day in the bush. They practically destroyed it and themselves and had lots of fun doing it, getting that need off the proverbial bucket list. One of them lost a shoe on an exhilarating ride. They had to retrace their steps to find it. You couldn't get too far with only one shoe, and who wants to wear their work boots when out on the town? After getting the bike into good running shape first, Garfield sold it. Carl mentioned in one of his letters that this was probably a good idea before someone got seriously hurt or worse. I don't think the gravel roads would have helped the situation.

In most of Carl's letters from camp he was trying to figure out how to get down to the country. In one, he mentioned that it took fourteen and a half hours getting down there, having to take the long way around by car. Nobody was getting much sleep on their days off back then—they seemed to be on the road too much. Not good for anyone's health, if you ask me. Young and foolish, the old folks would say. The price you pay for having a job and a girlfriend.

Carl and Garfield managed to catch a ride to Thunder Bay one weekend when the Lakehead Exhibition was in full swing. Boy, I sure wish I was along on that adventure. From what Carl told me, they enjoyed every minute of it. They went on every ride they had to offer and participated in all the games as well, losing money but still having fun. One of the adventures they encountered was a huge revolving culvert. The object was to crawl through it and come out the other end. When Garfield finally made it out, he had worn holes in the knees of his brand-new black pants. I smile now as I write this, picturing his bare knees peeking out through the holes.

I think this fun started out on a payday, but by the time they were back out of the gate, they found they had both spent their paycheques, or close to it. Boy, what a life! ENJOYING yourself, not worrying about tomorrow. Carl said he was so stiff and sore the following day that he could barely move, this being from all the rides they had been on. He ended up with a stuffed poodle dog to show for the money he had lost. This experience ended up being another fun thing to do while they were young that they could check off their bucket lists.

It wasn't all fun and games living in the bunkhouse, though. In another one of Carl's letters, he said that while he had been away for a weekend getaway, a drunken brawl had broken out and one of the members of the group had been locked up in the local jail and was still there. Sometimes men and booze just don't mix too well.

On another occasion, an older fellow that Carl had caught a ride with one time had a few too many with some still left to drink. He woke Carl up twice during the night to see if he wanted to join him for a beer. I guess by morning he had everyone awake. Poor old fellow! Just wanting someone to keep him company, I guess. Can't blame him for that! There's no company like your own. Except when you're drunk...

In another letter, Carl mentioned that the cook had been drunk for a week. What is it about living in the bunkhouse and drinking? When the men went for their lunch break it was supposed to be chicken stew on the menu. One of the workers took a ladle full of stew out of the pot and out came the dish rag with it! Carl said it spoiled the appetite. And it looked as if the dish rag had been cooked right along with the chicken. Lord, life in the bunkhouse wasn't without its downfalls, either. You sure couldn't plan on anything running smooth all the time, I suppose. In hindsight, this episode could be the reason why Carl wasn't fond of chicken...which I found out after we were married. There's a reason for everything, and if you dig deep enough, you'll usually find it.

Another letter, dated August 5, 1964, stated that they had taken a guy from Fort Frances to the hospital who had cut his leg with the chainsaw. Carl said he came out to where he was working with his belt tied around his leg to try to control the bleeding. He said it would be a long time before he would be returning to work as he had cut a piece of bone loose in his leg and the doctor had removed it. It was now sitting on his nightstand and his recovery was sure to take a while.

From another bunkhouse letter—gosh, I sure did like receiving them—he wrote about being on a trip to the Lakehead with Garfield in his car when they were stopped by the highway patrol. After pulling them over, the patrol gave them a warning not to do anything wrong around Atikokan. The patrol said they had heard about the guys around Stratton and that they "done whatever they wanted to, but they wouldn't get away with it in Atikokan." Good grief! And then some! That's a powerful reputation if I ever heard of one, or else somebody is being bullied. You be the judge. After all, I just copied it word for word from a letter and I believe it to be the truth, not a story that was made up.

Well, there was some good news for a change in a letter dated June 16, 1965: Carl wrote that the road from Fort Frances was finally open from 6 AM until 9 PM—for a while anyway. There was still some bridge work to be finished, but nevertheless, this would help the young men get home to the country without taking up so much of their precious time off. After this happened, they would take a car to the bridge and someone would meet them on the other side. They had to cross above the water by walking on a "gang plank," as Carl called it. This was a scary way to make their lives easier. And made for some careful planning...and talking to God before undertaking the walk! There was lots of fear, for sure.

Carl mentioned that one time he had to retrace his steps and offer encouragement to help a friend get across. Life just didn't seem to get easier for these young men, trying to make a living. Some of them had young families and a wife at home waiting for payday—the all-important factor that kept food on the table and gave the men the satisfaction of knowing their babies were being looked after.

The mail from the bunkhouse was delivered by the company airplane, so it didn't take long to get mail back and forth between home and the boys. Another notable incident Carl mentioned in a letter was a time when he caught a ride into town for the weekend and stayed with friends at their home. One morning when he awoke, he discovered that one of the sons in the family had cut a strip out of his hair down the centre of his head without waking him up. Now Carl enjoyed his hair and always kept it fixed "just so" with the curls dangling just the right way. You can imagine the dark purple hue in the room when he awoke and discovered what had gone down. Not a happy camper. After a trip to the barber to get it completely shaved off, it was then off to try and find a cap to fit his bald head, only taking it off at bedtime. I can just imagine the chore in that, especially now without any hair, it must have proven challenging to find a cap that actually fit!

It took a good six months for the hair to finally grow out enough, and of course an unforgiving attitude on his part towards the person responsible for this devastating hardship, as well. I was on Carl's side of the fence for this one—as I had to be seen out in public with him. Having no hair didn't suit Carl. Those sparkling blue eyes were lost without those blond curls hanging over his forehead.

The Bolen family farm.

Carl, sister Annie Armstrong, sister Kay Cameron, Brother Donald Bolen.

Carl standing in front of the bunkhouse at Camp 113.

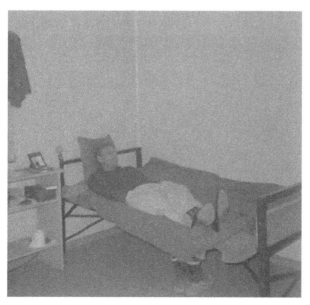

Carl, his bunk in the bunk house at Mando Camp #113.

Carl on the bike. Garfield sold it before they destroyed
it along with themselves. But it was fun!

Garfield Faragher Camp #113 Mando.

Carl Bolen Camp #113 Mando. Machine operator Paul Nikafortune.

Company Envelope used to mail letters.

Aug 11th 1964
Atikokan Ont

Dear Valerie
          Well got your letter
this morning so will answer
it this afternoon I have
lots of time we had to come
in from the bush at
noon yesterday and it was
still raining this morning
so we had to stay in today
to. I wish it had of waited
till Friday to rain I think,
Garfield is going to take his
car back down again it
took us 14½ hours to come
up here so will be on the
road just about all night
going down. Garfield just
sold his motorcycle to
another guy here in camp
just now so I guess the funs
over on that. We probably

would of wrecked it ourselfs
anyway. There's quite a few
here in camp after my poodle
dog but I'm going to hold
on to it. We were just figuring
out what time we would get
home if left after work on Friday
nite and we won't get their till
8 o'clock Saturday morning.
   I guess we'll go into the
bingo to-night theirs a $250.
jackpot maybe I'll be lucky
and win that. Well I'll
write a few more lines
to-morrow night it's supper
time now so I'll close this
and mail it in town so
it will go down on the train
to-morrow. Bye for now.
                    Love
                    Carl
                    x x x o o o o

Dec 6.th 1964
Atikokan Ont

Dear Valerie
        Well how goes everything
down their got the weekend
in here anyway its snowing
here to-day I sure hope
it warms up this week
it was 38 below here saturday
morning their was only three
of us in this bunkhouse this
weekend everybody else went
out. Their supposed to be a
guy try and drive across
the ice around the bridge
next week so if he can
make it we should be
able to get out of here the
next week-end. Well
Christmas is sure sneaking
up by the way what do
you want of Christmas

as far as I know yet we
have to work the day
before they did here last
year anyway. That old
guy I went down home
with last summer has been
drunk here all week-end
he woke me up a couple
times last night wanting
me to have a beer with him
he had just about everybody
in camp awake before
morning. Well as I say most
of the time can't think
of anything to write about
so bye for now hope to see
you soon.
        Love Carl
        xxxxxxxxx
        oo ooooooooo
I finally remembered your stamp

Letters from the bunk-house.

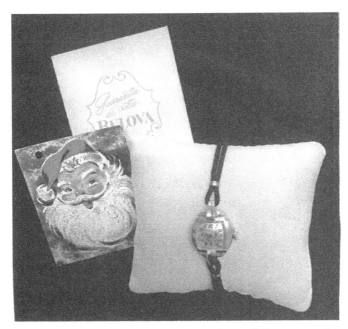

My first Christmas Gift, a Bulova Watch. Still dear to my heart!

The rings that came out of the glove box.

CHAPTER FIVE

Taking the Leap

We had come a long way from the first time I had caught a glimpse of Carl when I was still a young girl to our first "outing" together. This was to take place when I was babysitting, of course, on a Saturday night at my aunt's. I received a call that evening saying that he had permission to come and pick me up if I wanted to go to a friend's house where there was a gathering going on.

First, I had to get a replacement sitter. I asked a friend, Norman, who lived just down the road. He was kind enough to help me out. I had nothing suitable to wear, being this was unexpected. Norman, being a caring person, loaned me the gray sweatshirt he was wearing. Like I said before, people who lived in the country were always happy to help each other out when needed.

Getting back to our courtship days, after the one time of leaving my babysitting duties, the first real date was on another Saturday night. Carl called my parents' home and asked if I would like to go out that evening. Being raised with rather strict parents, I asked them for permission, needing to keep them on a happy playing ground with this courtship. First, I asked mother, who was busy in the kitchen. She was to say, "You'd better ask your dad." So off to the barn I ran, where he was busy with the cattle. His answer was, "What did your mother say?" I gathered from this comment that all was okay and so I ran back to the house and told Carl, "Yes, I can go." That first official date was to keep us happy for almost 53 years.

My sisters and I nicknamed our farmhouse "Wolverton Mountain" after a country song that was a hit at the time. Our house was built on a hill, and with all the girls in my family, the lyrics rather suited us—especially this line: "They say don't go on Wolverton Mountain if you're looking for a wife." Sort of reminds me of my sisters over the years choosing their husbands. Carl took the leap onto "Wolverton Mountain," being a young man on a mission.

Remember me mentioning the ring coming out of the glove box? That occasion happened on March 29, 1965, a surprise for me to say the least! And it was not expected in the middle of winter, as we had just experienced a huge snowstorm. Not your usual April romance happening here like most love stories. But nevertheless, it was to be ours.

Now we faced a new challenge: planning our big day and setting a date for the magic to happen. We agreed that the big event was to happen on September 17, 1965 and that day would be celebrated as our anniversary in the years to come. I would turn nineteen in August: a good age for a girl to face the hurdles of being a new wife and starting this "playing house" thing. Yes, let's get this show on the road! We started out by talking to the minister of Carl's boyhood church. Being that I worked in Nestor Falls and Carl in Atikokan, this was the only way we could start planning our big day.

We would hold the ceremony in the Shenston Lutheran Church just south of the Bolen farm. At this point in time it had been closed down and another church west of Stratton was being used for church purposes. After opening up the old family church with its many fond memories, getting it aired out, and ridding it of any dust and cobwebs that had accumulated over the years, it was finally all freshened up for the big day. We spoke to our minister, making final arrangements for our ceremony, and then he left to go on a summer vacation. The sad part was he never returned and the new minister who came to replace him didn't have a licence to marry in Canada. This was to be a huge setback for us, throwing the kibosh into our plans as we had our invitations printed and all set to mail out.

So began the search to find someone to marry us who wouldn't mind going into Carl's boyhood church. After a few visits and calls, we found a kind gentleman in Emo who was very understanding of our plight and more than happy to unite us. He was Reverend Fairbrother from the Baptist Church in Emo. This elderly gentleman showed us so much kindness and was never judgmental when dealing with the two of us.

Another minister we had visited during our search wanted to know why we wanted to get married in the first place. He was actually bold enough to ask me if I was in the family way, wondering if this could be the reason. Not caring for his attitude and also thinking that it was none of his business, I kindly informed him that we wouldn't be needing him. This caused his temper to flare up; but maybe he should have been a bit more thoughtful with his questions. Besides, Carl agreed with me.

Is this normal, or would it be like putting the cart before the horse? A wise bit of wisdom to say the least; and no, I wasn't in the family way. It probably would have made him sit back and peer over his glasses a little closer if I had told him the truth: I didn't have a clue in the first place just how babies were made! (I just had to throw this in here in case you're wondering—a little bit of shock therapy, you might say.) We didn't have that kind of a class when I went to school. We grew up in the dark you could also say. Farm girls didn't know everything, you see, even though we were brought up around animals that reproduced on a regular basis. My father made sure his girls lived a sheltered life and didn't get exposed to the "goings-on" in the barnyard. Anyway, I'd better let this rest before I get too worked up, being that I'm all alone and Carl is no longer here to share important matters with me and settle me down a notch.

Getting back to the big day, I'll always remember how handsome Carl looked in his custom-made suit which fit him in all the right places. The red tie he wore with his white shirt topped off those good looks, especially with his sparkling blue eyes and beautiful smile. By now his hair had grown back and the second crop was just as good as the first. It had come back to life nicely—after the hardship of having none for quite some time—as it slowly made its reappearance on his bald head.

I must also mention that look of love on his face was the best, especially that day, our wedding day. I noticed that his hand held mine just a little bit tighter. Finally, after all the courting and having fun on Saturday nights, we were a pair! No more going home alone at night, no more days or nights spent in the bunkhouse wishing he were somewhere else. Now we could dance whenever we wanted, take our own private road trips in the dark of night if we wanted to, listen to our country tunes whenever. Yes, the world was now ours to discover.

Thank you, Reverend Fairbrother, for making this happen and joining us together! It was a great honour to be married in Carl's boyhood church with all the special memories of Sundays past sharing our day! Speaking of Carl looking handsome on this important day, I thought I looked equally as good in my full-skirted white satin wedding gown with a large bow at the back waist. Of course, it had to be shortened to fit my four-foot eleven-inch height, but I felt like a princess in it. I had ordered it from the Eaton's catalogue while I was still working in Nestor Falls with no hopes of getting out to shop.

On our big day, Carl drove to Rainy River to pick up our flowers— yellow roses, my favourite colour. And after getting our hair done in Fort Frances, we were all set to go to the church. We had decorated the wedding cars with paper roses and streamers, a common practice back then. My girls who stood proudly by me were my sister, Sharon, my close cousin, Karen Johnson, and my special friend throughout our school days, Karen Advent. Wendy, my youngest sister, was my flower girl and the cutest in her old-fashioned dress with a little bustle, which was made by my mother. Everyone on my team was dressed in yellow to match my yellow roses, my favourite, and of course the colour scheme for the day. Carl had his brother Allan for best man, along with Sharon's boyfriend and future husband, George Halley, and also Carl's lifelong friend and soulmate, Garfield Faragher.

After a perfect wedding day ending with dinner and dancing, it was almost time for our grand finale. Of course, we had cut our wedding cake which was three tiers tall and decorated with yellow roses and white doves. This celebration was taking place at the Stratton Hall with Menard Whalen and his family playing the country music for the dance. They were a popular group back then and also made their home in Stratton. I can't recall anyone else ever playing for a dance there. The Stratton Hall was to our country village much like the Black Hawk

Hall was to Black Hawk, and was similar with the farm boys and girls getting together for their Saturday night dances. Putting farm life on hold for a night of fun!

They always had a large crowd who enjoyed listening to Menard sing as well as joining in the dancing at these events. A few favourite songs of mine that I remember and am still fond of were, "Old Dogs, Children and Watermelon Wine," "Tie a Yellow Ribbon Round the Old Oak Tree," and of course, "The Green, Green Grass of Home." He was very gifted, and we were very fortunate to have him included in our wedding day plans.

Now it was time for the celebration to come to a close. The speeches had been made. Now Carl had another important piece of paper in his possession: our certificate of marriage, signed, sealed, and ready for safe-keeping. We were finally married! Now we were all set to go forward on our journey together, learning new lessons in life. Carl had lost his freedom but didn't seem to mind. I was there to care for him, being his own private cook—no more dish rags in the stew! From now on it would be biscuits which turned out to be a favourite of his. There would be no more scrubbing his clothes on the washboard, either. (I remember from one of his letters that he had just finished his laundry and he thought there was a good possibility that his hands had come out cleaner than his laundry. From my memories of this chore, the scrub board could be a bit harsh on your knuckles also.) Oh! Those good old days! Somebody bring them back!

—————〰️∾ᴏᴏᴇᴛᴏᴏᴛᴇᴏᴏ〰️—————

This new journey of ours as husband and wife was going to be nothing that Carl and I couldn't handle as we had vowed, "in sickness or in health." We were more than ready to take it on, nothing to scare us here.

After we took our leave from the wedding and started out together, we had to find somewhere to spend our first night. This was to prove to be another hurdle. There was nothing to be had in Fort Frances, so we were to continue our search in International Falls until about four-thirty in the morning. We were fortunate enough to find a room in a rustic old hotel which was actually a bridal suite. By this time, it was beginning to be daylight and almost time for the rooster to start crowing.

In hindsight, maybe we should have planned this beforehand. But due to the fact that there was a certain amount of shyness here and there, we totally didn't deal with this important factor. We made sure everything was ready for our big day, but there were no plans made for our big night. Keep in mind that we are learning lots of lessons as we proceeded forward. Some were to be more important than others, if you can imagine.

The following day, after a short stay, we checked out of our hotel and headed back to the country once more, with Carl taking me to Barwick to meet his aunt Edith (a sister to his mom) and his uncle Pete Stewart along with their son Marvin. Edith was bedridden, crippled with rheumatoid arthritis and couldn't attend our wedding celebration. This was another glimpse of the kindness and caring, always thinking ahead, that Carl showed when it came to people less fortunate. (Later in life, he was stricken with this same ailment which took a toll on his health, with him suffering for years with the pain caused from this debilitating disease. Also, the medications used to treat this were harsh and not without nasty side-effects. There were to be many trips to Thunder Bay to see specialists who could hopefully help him through all this.)

Proceeding on to the farm, we spent the afternoon opening our wedding gifts. After spending the night at Carl's father's home, we set out on a road trip to Thunder Bay to spend some time with his sister, Kay, her husband, Alex Cameron, and their daughters, Leslie and Tammy.

The trip was beautiful with all the hills in the area alive with their fall colours. This memory is still very dear to me, not having enjoyed seeing such vivid oranges and reds before this. The Thunder Bay area, seemingly mountainous, was a blanket of beautiful colours lighting up the hillsides along the highway.

While in Thunder Bay, I was fortunate enough to meet some of Carl's mother's family, the Andrews. As I mentioned, they all had musical backgrounds and enjoyed playing all the good old-time music makers: fiddles, guitars, accordions, and other instruments they made themselves. Carl was anxious that I got to meet his Uncle Les whom he talked fondly of and who enjoyed singing as well.

In all the years of being with Carl he never lost his ability to put a name to a singer who was singing a country music song on the radio. He never lost his love of good old country music, and his love of dancing.

Our honeymoon came to an end and it was time to settle down to our life together as man and wife. We were fortunate to find an apartment on Abbott Road, so we moved our meagre belongings and set up house. It was one long room with a bed at one end and kitchen at the other. It proved to be very open concept by today's standards: the cupboards had no doors, and for cooking, only a hotplate. The bathroom outside the door contained only a toilet, nothing else.

Our first purchase was a galvanized wash tub to enable us to enjoy a bath as often as possible. Then the next big buy was a wringer washer, a major treat for sure, but very much needed. No more sore knuckles from the washboard. This was bought at Eaton's and on a payment plan of seven dollars a month, which was a good deal of money back in 1965. Buying this also gave us another important piece of paper, our first credit card, which we used for many other purchases in the years to come. This was another piece of paper for Carl to keep tucked safely in his wallet.

I don't know what my thoughts were on this apartment, though. People tried to make a dollar wherever they could from whatever space they weren't using. But then again, I suppose someone out there was sure to appreciate a roof over their head and a bed in the corner to lie down on…that's what I was thinking.

The cooking in this place proved to be a challenge as well, with only a hot plate—no oven. I recall making a lemon pie and trying to brown the meringue in an electric fry pan, a new invention back then, and having no luck. It proved to be difficult to show my cooking skills to my new husband without having an oven, that's for sure!

On one of our visits down to the country after we were married, Carl's father gifted me with two of his wife's cookbooks. I was sitting in the living room and he came out of the kitchen carrying them, saying he wanted me to have them. One of them was *The Blue Ribbon*

Cookbook. The other, *A Guide to Good Cooking*, was compiled by the makers of Five Roses Flour. They had been Mrs. Bolen's when she was busy feeding her family, canning and baking and spoiling them all. I was overwhelmed by this act of kindness, and had a difficult time fighting back the tears. What a beautiful way of saying welcome to our family, to give me something that had belonged to his wife. He was a kind man and this gesture meant a great deal to me. Both of the cookbooks are old and well worn, back from the time when wood was used for cooking and baking, or coal, also mentioned, would have been used as well. The pages are thin and falling apart, but I will still always cherish them. For many Christmases to come, I always made a recipe for plum pudding for Carl from one of them.

Carl missed having a proper sink for his manly chore of shaving. He had to contend with sitting at the kitchen table with a bowl of hot water and a mirror propped up so he could see what was happening. Yes, this was to be our new life until the following year when we found a small house on McKenzie Avenue for rent. It was no more than a shack, having been skidded in from the Mando Camps, but at least it had two bedrooms and its very own bathroom, with a toilet, sink, and a bathtub.

Our accommodations were starting to improve. We rented this for seventy-five dollars a month, a fair amount back then. This new home had a huge living room which could have been a screened-in porch in earlier years. It had a space heater in the living room which ran on fuel oil, not my favourite mode of heating, having gotten used to and liking wood heat. There was no comparison between the smell of fuel oil and wood smoke, that's for sure!

Something that I distinctly recall from this house when we first moved in was the ceilings. They were covered in brown specks of fly poop. This was something I never saw before, even after having lived on the farm with flies of every nature buzzing around. It was to take lots of elbow grease to clean everything up, plus a few gallons of paint.

Life wasn't full of perks, but at least we were together. It was better than our dating years when we couldn't see each other as often as we had wanted. That had been a lonely part of our life, for sure. We could handle a few inconveniences to just be together, remembering from Carl's letters that he missed me and wished I were there. It was the same when I worked at Crow Lake in Nestor Falls. I could understand the boys taking a chance on getting caught by the CNR police if it was the only way to get home. At that point, our time together was very limited, so this new life of ours was all good. As long as we were together, there were no complaints.

Our Wedding day – Sept 17, 1965.

Stratton Hall at our reception.

The Bridal Party
Left: Garfield Faragher, George Halley, Allen Bolen, Right:
Sharon Schram, Karen Johnson, Karen Advent. Centre: Mr. Carl
and Mrs. Valerie Bolen, Front: Wendy Schram, flower girl.

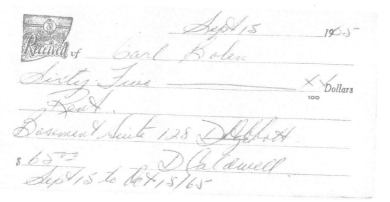

Rent on our first apartment, 128 Abbot Rd.

Carl on his way to work at Mando.

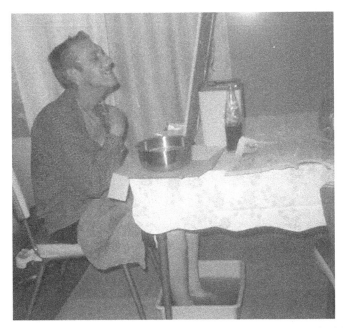

Shaving at the kitchen table. "making do with what we had!"

Carl, enjoying dish duty.

Carl with a friend Ralph Haney.

The Pontiac Carl bought before we were married.

Carl and Ralph's stock car that they tuned up for
the Atikokan Stock Car club races.

Carl's Pontiac after someone drove through a yield sign.

Melbourne Shrumm, Robert Bolen (dad) Beach Shrumm, and Carl.

CHAPTER SIX

If Walls Could Talk

We weren't living very long at our new address on McKenzie Avenue when we got our boarders. I mentioned previously, at that time my life was to get somewhat challenging for a short while.

And then something devastating happened which tore at our heart strings once again. One of Carl's good buddies and co-workers, Alex, who had also worked in the bush, lost his life on the job. Carl found out about Alex's fear of water when going down to the country, before the bridge was completed. Alex was the one who froze up when crossing the "gang plank" and Carl had to go back and pry his fingers loose and get him across to safety and his family.

Prior to the time of his death, Alex had a disagreement with the company for not paying the men for showing up in the bush for work. If it rained or otherwise and they were unable to work that day, the men were sent home for the shift with no pay for their time spent travelling to work. At this time, Alex had filed a complaint with the union, and the company responded by sending him to the Fort Frances area to work on the water gathering logs to float to the mill. I think it was called a "log boom" or something of that nature. He was wearing a brand-new pair of boots that day; whether or not that had something to do with him slipping and falling into the water, no one can be sure. He lost his life that day. As I recall the company was aware of his fear of water. He didn't want to go to this new job site and couldn't understand why he was being sent there. "Was this a way to punish me?" he was thinking.

He confided in Carl before he was to go, and this was the only reason he could think of. The evening before he left for Fort Frances, he actually spent the night in his car parked in our driveway on McKenzie Avenue, unable to sleep with all the worries engulfing his thoughts. We were not aware of him until morning, or Carl would have brought him into the house and made sure he went to bed and that his fears were settled.

Alex Patterson was gone too early, leaving behind a young family who would face the future without their father. His sister Sylvia Brandrick still lives in Atikokan. I hope by putting my pen to Alex's story it will somehow pay tribute to him, honour him in some small way as a special friend, a good teammate on the job, a kind man.

"God Bless you Alex."

Alex

After losing his friend and co-worker, Carl quit his job working for Mando. In 1966, shortly after the death of Alex, Carl began to work for the Caland Ore Company. He was a labourer for some time, shovelling the red dirt onto a conveyor belt where it went to the plant to be made into pellets. I trust this information is correct.

We were soon blessed with another boarder from Stratton: Roger Bolen, a son of Carl's cousin. He had found work at the mine after he had graduated from high school. We enjoyed having him live with us and were happy to let him have a room in our little home. He was always happy-go-lucky and was easy to care for. It was a great way for Carl to get to know more of his family. They lived in Shenston as well, only two miles north of Carl's family home. I have to mention a favourite lunch of Roger's—he enjoyed raw onion sandwiches! See what I mean about being easy to care for? He would even make them himself. He had another quirk which was sucking on lemons to keep himself awake on the drives from Atikokan to Shenston for his days off. He ended up falling in love with an Atikokan girl. After their wedding, they moved to Eastern Ontario to work for Ontario Hydro, I believe. We enjoyed Roger's company and were glad to have him while he lived in Atikokan.

Our next boarder was my brother, Dennis, who came to our doorstep the same evening that he graduated from Rainy River High School. He, along with a friend of his, came to town eager to work and found a job at Caland Ore the next day. It was off to Walt's store to get outfitted with proper work clothes, eager to start work and be put on the payroll. Dennis ended up staying with us for a few years through the birth of our first daughter, Carla, and on.

Before I was "done" I'm thinking that I had all my brothers staying in our home at one time or another on McKenzie Avenue West. We even had my father stay with us for a short while when he was working for George Armstrong on the highway outside of town. This was another pleasure for us, cooking and packing lunches for my dad. Yes, the door was always open at our little house on McKenzie and we were happy to welcome our family and friends when they needed a place to rest their heads.

We had the pleasure of having Carl's father stay with us also. He was staying with two of his sons, Allan and Raymond, while they were working for John Stewart in the Crilly area cutting wood. While staying with them in a "shack" in the bush, he ended up sick and was hospitalized in Atikokan. This occurred in the early winter of 1966. Not liking hospitals, the nurses called me one day to come over and see if I could settle him down. Apparently, he was wanting out of there.

This didn't surprise me as I had been told by one of his sons that he had broken a leg while working in the bush when he was eighty years old and had signed himself out of the hospital, even though he wasn't well enough to go home. To make a long story short, he came home with me that day the nurse called. I looked after him on McKenzie Avenue until he was well enough to go back to Crilly, which is in the Seine River area.

Our little house on McKenzie had lots of stories to tell (if it could talk!) That's the truth. There seemed to be something going on all the time. It's a wonder when I think back on it, that I got any sleep in those early years of our marriage. When Mr. Bolen ended up at his own home in Shenston once more, Carl and I would visit him often to check on him and help out as much as possible. He was nearly blind by this time.

I would have to thread a needle for him just in case he might have something to sew. He would have it out ready for me. That seemed to be a priority of his. He would also have a pot of potatoes peeled and ready, sitting on the back of the stove, ready to start cooking, eager to feed us. He had another habit which was climbing the stairs at night to check and see if we were in bed. We could hear him slowly making his way up, stopping and peeking in the doorway before making his way back down the stairs to where his own bed was.

He was soon to move in with another son of his, Donald, and Donald's wife, Stella, who lived close by, just across the road from Mr. Bolen's house on the family farm where he had been living alone. At this time, his health had been failing and he was to pass away in February, 1967, at the age of eighty-four years old.

After his passing, whenever Carl and I spent the night at the farm, we could still hear him painstakingly making his way up the stairs at night, just as he used to when he was still with us, checking on his boy, making sure he was in his bed and safe for another day. Once you are a parent, you never forget. You'll always be a parent, keeping your children safe even when you are in heaven.

Mr. Bolen was a good parent, one to be proud of. He was well-respected by his friends and family. He was now happy, reunited with his loving wife who left him too early at the age of fifty-seven years old in 1954. Carl had told me that when she was still alive, his father never left her side, sitting beside her and keeping her company if she was knitting or sewing. No wonder he was so broken without her. Their life was truly a love story. With all of the pain and loss they had suffered over the years, they were always there to comfort each other and offer support through the sad times.

During all of this sadness, Carl was still working at Caland Ore Company where they had left him too long as a labourer, he thought. This is where the new hired men start out and my opinion on this was that they were actually getting some work done for a change, something they weren't used to from someone on a shovel handle. Eventually he was operating a front-end loader, loading iron ore into the trucks that would haul it to the pellet plant where it would be crushed and made into iron ore pellets before it was shipped to Thunder Bay.

Carl always put 100% into any job he undertook, so he most likely put forth a good effort labouring on the shovel handle. One thing you could never refer to him as being was a "useless tool" when it came to his work ethics. I had to use that word, picking it up on my journey with him. It means not being worth your salt, or paycheck in this case. The foreman at that time accused him of sticking the shovel into the belt causing a work stoppage. After numerous accusations, Carl finally lost his patience, putting him in his place! The foreman never accused him of anything after that. I still remember what he said to him, and you can bet that it got his attention.

I got the feeling later on that my man wasn't happy working here. He always worked hard at what he signed up for, but just didn't care for foremen with attitude problems. The red dust didn't help matters, either. I must say that I was behind him on this. Don't try to break a good work horse's spirit; you'll get what you deserve. I know this for sure from my farm days. When a horse kicks, they mean business; you'd best not be standing too close when this happens. (Much the same as kicking a good dog once too often. There is nothing worse than seeing an abused dog slinking around with his tail between his legs, afraid of people.)

So, don't try and take the spunk out of my little man. There! I feel better now. It pays to take the apron off and straighten problems out, keep things in line. It's also a good lesson for some of the superiors out there. Don't forget who is responsible for putting butter on your bread. If it weren't for the hard-working men out there, your bread could end up being quite dry if I've got anything to say. It doesn't hurt to let your man know that you are behind him in his daily chore of trying to make a living and support his family.

I mentioned before that our little house on McKenzie was always bustling with something happening steady it seemed. It was always buzzing, busier than a beehive without the pleasure of having the honey. Yes, it just never stopped. We enjoyed lots of company in those early years, with no shortage of activities going on. It was just a good thing that Carl and I were there for anyone needing a place to roost for the night.

In particular, his brothers who I mentioned would make an occasional trip into town from Crilly to attend to business. And more important, they'd come to curb their hankering for a good cold beer, wash the sawdust from their throats, and while they were at it, forget to stop until closing time or last call.

We used to await their return, peeking out the living room window to watch for their grand arrival. We would kneel on the chesterfield and peer down the street for a glimpse, knowing the time they should be appearing. You can only imagine the trail they were blazing on this journey to our home. We both enjoyed this picture, two drunken sailors soon to be at our door.

After getting them safely into the house (sometimes the doorsteps caused a few problems especially for these two boys who were unsteady on their feet), the next thing would be to sit back and watch them try to remove those proverbial green rubber boots from their feet. This could cause quite a commotion on occasion. I distinctly remember the night one of the brothers lost his balance during the course of this chore and didn't get stopped until going clean across the living room floor! He stopped only when he had crashed into the space heater, jarring loose the pipes. The stove was almost taken off its moorings, and I will say that if the pipes needed the soot cleaned from them before, they didn't now. No, it wasn't the best way, though maybe the messiest, for getting the stove pipes cleaned. (After having wood heat on the farm, I never did care for this method of heating our home in the first place.)

Another incident I must share with you while telling stories of the brothers happened on a Sunday morning. After a Saturday night of not having them break their proverbial trail to our doorstep, a knock came on our door late the next morning. When Carl opened it, in stepped one of the boys in blue and behind him one of the brothers, being escorted by the officer, with a sheepish look on his face.

The officer had brought him from the local lock-up and he needed a little thing called bail money. That was the problem, and this explained why we did not have the pleasure of their company the previous night. They had been provided with a different bunk the night before. It was sort of like staying at a grand hotel minus a comfortable bed, with bars on the windows so you had no chance of escaping—even if the thought had maybe crossed your mind. They had been involved in an encounter at a local hot spot where you could enjoy a good meal after your thirst had been quenched.

The cause of this incarceration was the fact that one of the brothers had fallen asleep at this establishment and the other brother had been asked to wake him up and continue on their merry way. The awake one couldn't get anywhere with this request, not being able to rouse the sleeping beauty. Sleep can come easy after a hard day working in the bush and then partaking in a few cold ones. This sets the stage for a good long nap, which I can see happening here. Failing to reach an agreement and trying to negotiate with the business owner, who by now was losing his patience, the brother that was still awake tried to make a point by hitting the glass display counter with his fist—shattering it! This prevented all hopes of this encounter ending on a good note.

The moral of this story is maybe you should have a good snack first before taking on a beer drinking marathon. (Sorry brothers. I love you to death, but that was surely just a case of poor planning.)

The story ended with Carl accompanying the two visitors to the local lock up and paying for this little misadventure. I am sure it took a cord or two of pulp wood to replace the thick glass countertop. That was all part of the deal before the handcuffs came off. The hand that was used to make a point needed a bit of first aid as well as some iodine.

Another unsettling time for me was on a different night when the boys blessed us with their company once again. On this particular occasion, Carl was working the night shift and I was left alone to deal with these two characters in question. They had come to town once again from Crilly to handle their important business. They honoured us with a sleepover which ended up being what I'm going to call a farm boys' pajama party. I was to be entertained by one of the two of them running around the house in his one-piece long woolen underwear. (You know what I'm talking about and may have even had a pair yourself back in the day. The kind with the trap door in the back end which you kept buttoned up to keep out that chilly north wind. Also, if I'm thinking right, after washing them, they usually had to hang on the clothesline for a week before you could safely say they were dry. I recall a pair of my father's hanging on the line and a little brown Jenny Wren making a nest in them. A nice cozy place to raise her babies, for sure!)

With this brother issue, it ended up being an evening spent with me trying to get this lad to stay in bed and hopefully go to sleep. This was to prevent him from hurting himself, being a bit unsteady on his feet, which was a usual happening. I wasn't ready just yet to have the pipes jarred loose anytime soon. Soot can make a mess that I wasn't wanting to have to clean up again.

In the course of events with the brothers, I was to learn that sometimes that "OLD V" seemed to keep you awake, and other times it could put you into a deep sleep. This brother was quite busy that night, "hyperactive" you could say. Yes, you could always count on them to be entertaining. They lived a colourful life for sure. One of the brothers used to describe himself as "tighter than a new boot," knowing full well what the problem was.

About this time, my family doctor was trying to figure out why my blood pressure was a bit high. Maybe he should have spent some time at our home, then he could have witnessed with his own eyes what some of the probable causes could be. Carl and I were more than happy to give his brothers a place to stay, at least a bed for them to sleep in when they were in town on one of their adventures. They weren't hard to look after once they were settled in their beds for the night. They never had too much of an appetite in the mornings, only needing a few good cups of coffee to settle them down before heading back to their bunkhouse in the wilds.

I could see a pattern happening with this life, making a living in the bush and being away from civilization. The men who had the pleasure of this lifestyle were always happy to get away for a few days to spread their wings, whether it was to visit a girlfriend and curb their loneliness or to take a trip to an establishment to curb their thirst with a good cold drink and to meet up with friends.

Life back then was what you made it, and how you made the boring times come to life was another story. This new chapter in my life of being newly married was certainly an eye opener. And made me aware that, yes, maybe I did have a sheltered life after all when I was growing up.

My father had a certain manner of looking at you in a disbelieving way, and he would shake his head at you if your actions were unusual or surprised him in some way. I'm sure he would have been doing that quite often these days. He didn't have to speak, it was just that look from under his eyebrows, his way of showing his disapproval. I must say he was big on common sense.

When all is said and done, Carl's brothers knew how to do things up, I must say. They certainly could spoil their own fun without too much planning. After all the tragedy in their lives, they deserved to enjoy happiness wherever they could find it. Life is short enough as it is.

CHAPTER SEVEN

Trying Times

I must tell you another story of Carl that I've been saving for a rainy day. Speaking of rain or water, he never cared to go fishing. He never cared to eat fish either, which ties into my theory. I can think of two possible reasons. One being that he had lost a good friend due to drowning in a work-related accident. Another possible reason was that he was nauseated just from thinking about fish because in his younger days, working outside the home, he was served a big pot of boiled suckers for lunch. This incident had turned him off eating fish. One of the things that I was learning about Carl was the fact that he had a powerful memory and didn't forget something as traumatic as this. The home where this was served could have been folks who were lucky they had anything at all to eat back in the day. In tough times you made do with whatever you had in order to stay alive. It was wartime, and the depression was extremely difficult on the housewives of that era, especially with the food rations. Yes, surviving wasn't easy back then. If it didn't kill you, it definitely made you grow up to be a stronger person, thankful for what you had. No matter if it scared you for life or not.

When it came to hunting, in the early years Carl enjoyed getting out into the forest with his buddies for that evasive moose. He didn't have the pleasure of this hunt in Stratton; there just didn't seem to be any of these creatures living and having families in this region. The geological area didn't provide the habitat that was necessary for moose.

It was farming country and lacked all the swamp areas that moose enjoy and need for foraging for survival.

He enjoyed taking his big gun with him—the two-man deal—with one man having to hold it and aim and the other pulling the trigger. It had belonged to his Uncle Tom and sort of reminded me of "Uncle Tom's Cabin." It was the cause of much laughter between him and Garfield on one of their hunting trips. I also recall much bruising on their shoulders. As long as they had fun making their memories without losing an eye to this sport, all was okay!

I remember one hunt when they actually returned with a moose along with all the excitement of using the big gun. I do recall that it was a bull moose, and of course we were still living on McKenzie Avenue where all the craziness and memories were happening. The men were busy dismembering this animal, and I was standing at the screened-in kitchen door watching. All of a sudden there was a loud splat on the doorstep in front of the door where I was standing. Carl called out and asked me if I wanted to keep this part, this thing he had just thrown down. Of course, there was much laughter from the hunters and an equal amount of embarrassment from me. This is when I knew it was a bull moose! Now that I was up on things...

No, I didn't want it, but after thinking it over later, I probably could have thrown it into a pot for his supper. Yes, that little cutie pie had lots of nerve and deserved something in retaliation: something else to put in his bucket list of things you shouldn't do. It most likely would have turned him off eating moose as well as chicken and fish, I'm thinking. When the boys got together for a hunt, they enjoyed themselves and made many lasting memories.

I'm thinking that I got my revenge for this bit of humiliation later, on a night when I sat at the kitchen table with a broom in my hand for a good part of the night. I had pulled open the drawer beneath the oven on the stove and discovered that someone had been into my Christmas candy and was storing it out of sight, or so they thought. I enjoyed my Christmas hard candy mix just like Carl and Mickey had enjoyed their peppermints, so I couldn't let this go on. If there was a mouse in this house, it had to go. You could never guess all the places it could investigate in the cover of night when it thought it was safe to explore.

So, I set my plan in action and waited at the table, hoping to get a glimpse of this small-scale thief. Lo and behold, he made an appearance scooting across the kitchen floor! At that same exact time, I brought that broom down so hard on this little creature that Carl jumped out of bed wondering what on earth had happened. Scared the daylights out of him, so I did!

But after finding out that I had only killed a mouse and that the roof wasn't caving in on top of him like he thought, he went back to bed. I was left to deal with the carcass, and being afraid to touch it, I swept it up with the broom and tossed it out the door. I slept good that night after my heart stopped beating so hard, not having to worry about a furry little creature crawling around in bed with us.

Gosh, the things a farm girl has to contend with living in this town. It was starting to be a real eye opener, for sure. Reality was beginning to set in, as I was busy now cleaning and scrubbing, not wanting to leave any traces of a mouse that had the run of our house. In other words, no mouse pee was going to be left behind, or Christmas hard-mixed candy either, which was sad for me to think about. I don't think the good old-fashioned kind is even made anymore—the kind Santa used to put in your candy bag to enjoy after your Christmas concerts at the Pattullo #8 School. A memory dear to my heart.

Now I'll tell you about another little incident that left a trace of annoyance on my special little man's face. This happened on another occasion when he was trying to sleep. I see a pattern happening here, now that I stop and think about it. It was daytime and Carl was working the night shift, with one more to go. We were going to head down to the country for some rest and relaxation and fresh farm air. At the end of one of our trips, we came home to find that someone had slept in our house while we were away, as they needed a bed and a friend of Carl's had invited them to stay at our home. How friendly can you be? After this incident, I always had this on my mind whenever I was planning to leave town. From then on, I made sure the house was in good order, very tidy and all that good stuff, just in case.

The next thing that happened here was almost difficult for me to believe, not only Carl. It was one of those times when I had to give my own head a shake. I made up my mind to clean the bedroom while

Carl was sound asleep in bed. You can probably guess what's coming next. I decided to move the bed over and damp mop under it. No dust balls would be left behind for some stranger to see and store in his memory bank. If anything was going to be stored, it would be the thought that I was such a good housewife and how clean and fresh the house was. Anyway, to my surprise—and Carl's—the bed fell apart with him sleeping in it! Not a happy camper. No words were needed. Just to be jarred from a deep sleep was enough of a shock, especially when you were now on the floor and not sleeping like a baby in your bed. This, I'm quite sure, was enough to break the proverbial camel's back. No straw needed here. It didn't take him long to get up onto his feet and head to the other bedroom to see if he could get back to that place where he was enjoying a nice sleep. It wouldn't have surprised me if he was beginning to wonder if he had made the right choice taking me on for a wife! They say you learn by making mistakes, and by then I was on a roll.

It's just a good thing that my doctor didn't get wind of this latest adventure. At that time, he was treating me for high blood pressure and was trying to determine what could be the possible cause. He asked me if I had a cleaning disorder, asking about the doorknobs, for example. He wondered if I washed them daily, maybe even more than once. I didn't bother to tell him that I had an issue with floors. I liked them to be clean and polished at all times. Carl would be the first to agree with this assessment.

What I needed was some little bare feet running around to keep me busy and lower my energy to a manageable level. Maybe then Carl could get the rest he needed, that his body required, to enable him to work at the pace he enjoyed. I would be kept occupied and not have the time to cause sudden crashes that seemed to be keeping him from sleep. God bless him and what he had to put up with—nothing he had planned on, I'm sure. One thing: he had a strong heart. The doctor had told him so, which was a blessing for sure.

This floor addiction was getting out of control. Even I could see this. On another occasion to do with floors, I was scrubbing and waxing them. Of course, you had to wait awhile for the wax to dry before you could walk on them. This was to be a tedious job which I would do on my hands and knees; but it was all worthwhile when you saw the nice clean, shiny results.

Meanwhile, Carl was bored and was pacing around the house, so I kindly asked him if he minded sitting for a while so I could finish my floors. He agreed to go for a walk to pick up the mail which would take care of this little problem. Off he went to get the mail; this was about eleven o'clock in the morning. I never saw him again till that evening when, lo and behold, the front door flew open and there stood Carl, teetering on the doorstep. He hollered out and asked if the floor was dry. Boy, it's sure a good thing that the Grey Goose Bus didn't go by our house back then, for I'm afraid I may have hopped on it. And think of all the fun I would have missed out on if that had happened!

Anyway, I did my duty and got him safely into the house and helped him lie down on the chesterfield, which was close to the door...thank goodness. I distinctly remember that his arm was dangling down, he had his hand on the floor, probably to stop the room from spinning. There was no going to work that night. We got around the problem by fibbing to his boss telling him Carl was sick and wouldn't be able to work that night.

Checking my memory bank, this was the first and last time he would try this little trick. Probably realizing the hurt he was causing— mainly to my heart. Especially over a small incident like this! So much for showing appreciation for all the care that I put into keeping our mouse-infested house neat and tidy...and free from rodents. I thought that I was doing such a good job of things, what with cooking his favourite meals and everything else a wife will do to impress her man.

I enjoyed my new role and didn't think I was doing too bad so far and didn't deserve any whiplash from what I could see. Maybe I needed to start reading a few copies of the *Woman's Home Journal* or something. Get some new ideas where I could improve my performances around the house. That would surely shock him into thinking that I wasn't doing too bad a job with all my washing and waxing and things like that.

In hindsight, maybe I could have planned my moves better, not trying to do too much cleaning and moving things around when Carl was home. Save it for when he was working, might be the best idea for both of us. Also, the evening he came home from his outing and I had to help him into the house certainly brought back memories. I had practice with this chore when his brothers would pay us those late-night visits, teetering on the doorstep.

After these small mishaps, I think I may have evened the score over that little thing relating to the bull moose. Maybe I will put this to rest and keep my hopes up that nothing else will cause me this kind of distress again. After all, Carl was still the same man who stood in the church beside me, just a bit mischievous at times.

CHAPTER EIGHT

Being a Daddy

It was near the end of my final tree planting season that I had some exciting news for Carl. I can still see the look on his face. He had been shaving, a chore of his that I enjoyed watching, with his face all soaped up and the sound of his razor being pulled across his face, removing the prickles of whiskers that seemed to appear like magic overnight. After he was finished with this routine, I told him the news.

He was going to be a Daddy! I still remember the big smile that lit up his face with happiness! The first comment from him, after hearing this news was, "Now I'll go to work to buy booties." He was looking forward to being a new father, and we were both impatient for the big day to arrive.

This new event in our lives took place on April 4, 1969. After an ambulance trip to the Port Arthur General Hospital in Thunder Bay, our first little girl was born who we named "Carla Rae" after her Daddy and her Uncle. For all the troubles we had on her journey into the world, she showed signs of being very mature for her age. She was the only newborn in the nursery who was wide awake, looking around, and checking out her surroundings.

This first daughter of ours was a good baby, a little lady with a cheery attitude; there was to be no colic or walking the floors at night, or anything of that nature that could stress out new parents to the limit. I must also add that on the night of her birth, while I was on the way to the hospital in the ambulance, Carl beat us there in his car. Wow! I'm happy I wasn't riding with him at the time, that's for sure.

Carl's brothers were very proud to be uncles and came to visit us after we arrived back to Atikokan with our new daughter, bringing some other friends with them. Her Uncle Raymond gave her a pink teddy bear. She loved this bear and later chewed on it, removing one of the eyes and almost choking on it. On my way out to hang the wash, I heard her coughing. I went back to check on her, thinking she was getting a cold…this was to be a reality check for us. She was only five months old when this happened, and after getting the pieces, five in all, I removed the other eye and took it apart to see if I had it all or not. Yes, she now had a pink teddy bear with no eyes. It's like many other things back then—this was extremely hazardous and could have had a different ending. From that day forward, we kept a close eye on things.

At the time of Carla's birth, her father wasn't working; whether it was a lay off or a strike, I'm not sure. He was planning on leaving town, looking for a new job with a paycheque attached. Now with a new girl to provide for, the worry was beginning to set in. Not wanting him to leave, and without telling him, I phoned my previous boss on the tree planting crew to see if there was a chance for me to get a job instead. He told me to catch the bus in the morning; I could have a job if I wanted. At this time Carla was barely four weeks old, so for me it was quite a challenge stumbling around in the bush, but at least it provided an income and I was happy about that fact.

Carl in the meantime was the Mom and Dad, staying at home taking care of his little girl, feeding her and whatever else comes with looking after a four-week-old baby. I knew there would be nothing to worry about leaving him with this prestigious job.

He was a kind and gentle father and made a good home for his girls over the years. We were blessed with another daughter almost four years later. Corina Dawn was premature and seemed to have everything children are prone to get before she was a year old: measles, mumps, chicken pox, and finally in August of that year, the whooping cough, which was going around in the Rainy River area at that time. She certainly didn't thrive very well at the start. Because of her being ill so much, she didn't get her regular immunization shots until she was probably a year old. There were times with the whooping cough when I didn't think she was going to survive. The doctor wouldn't hospitalize her at the time, saying she would get better care at home. I was left wondering about this; I was not trained to be a nurse by any means. When this nightmare was over, I had my doubts and was feeling lucky to have survived myself. There certainly was to be little sleep on the horizon.

One night when she was turning blue from choking and coughing and unable to breathe, I panicked and actually ran outside with her. At times I would also run cold water on her to see if she would gasp and get her breath back. To say the least, it was to be a living hell and I would question the doctor's reasoning today. The hospital is for sick people, including babies. I feel extremely lucky that she even survived this ordeal. She was only seven months old at the time and was very small for her age due to health problems, including the childhood diseases and being allergic to milk which caused her a lot of distress when it came to thriving and being a happy baby.

Our firstborn, Carla, was born on Good Friday and I was to spend Easter in the hospital. Along with this came a visit from the Easter Bunny. Corina, not be outdone, was born late in the evening on December 23, 1972, so I was to spend Christmas in the hospital with her. Along with this came a visit from Santa Claus. As I said before, Carl planned his moves for sure. What more could you want? Two gifts from heaven for him. We had an Easter egg and a Christmas present.

He enjoyed raising his girls, treating them with gentle hands, respect, and dignity. He was always careful to let them make their own decisions through their growing up hurdles, much the same as he himself had been raised. He offered them advice only if they needed or wanted it. To my way of thinking, he was a perfect father. This was to be a goal of his, trying to do his best whatever he was up to, like working in the bush for example, giving his job 100%.

After all the fun and enjoyment of the years of living on McKenzie Avenue, we decided, after I hinted of course, that maybe it was the right time to buy a house for us to live in. Carl enjoyed his new cars but now with the two little girls it seemed like a good idea to own a house, somewhere for them to play outside and have fun. Besides, it was close to ten years that we had been renting.

I guess he agreed with this bit of wisdom, and so soon we were moving to our first home on 101 Black Road, in the Lone Pine area. This was a two-bedroom house on a large corner lot; plenty of room for the girls to play and also a place to plant a garden. Carl built a picket fence around the property and painted it white. He let the girls choose the paint colour for the house and they picked pink for the house with cherry trim. It looked quite nice if I do say so myself, and it was to be our stamp on it. Kay was a nurse at St. Joseph's Hospital in Thunder Bay at the time, and one of her patients from Atikokan told her that there must have been a sale on pink paint.

Carl built new kitchen cupboards in the garage and moved them into the house for my birthday. He took lots of time planning and building the cupboards, making a butterfly style to go around the kitchen window. I can also recall him measuring cereal boxes as he wanted to make sure they could be stood up in the cupboard. The countertop he used was also carefully cemented on to the kitchen table; then I recovered the kitchen chairs so they matched. We both thought it looked just great when it was completed.

Our backyard was always busy with neighbourhood children playing until dark with some of their parents having to come looking for them when it was time to call it a day for playtime. Oftentimes, I would supply snacks for this hungry bunch. They enjoyed my homemade pancakes rolled up with butter and sprinkled with sugar. This kept me busy at the stove trying to keep up to the kids waiting patiently at the door for a hot pancake. It was like they had their own marathon going on! And back then sugar wasn't such a bad thing for them like they think it is today. At least it didn't seem to hurt my girls that I noticed along the way of their growing up.

Speaking of the backyard, Carl put up a swing set for the playing and having fun stuff. This also came with a slide that the younger ones enjoyed. He also built a sturdy teeter-totter for their enjoyment. They had lots of fun on this, even though there were a few small injuries if the weight wasn't properly balanced. By this I mean when someone would get the bright idea of jumping off, which would send the smaller one airborne.

The girls enjoyed playing with their friends. And speaking of Carl, he let them make their own decisions, as I mentioned earlier. He wouldn't say, "It's time to come inside now and have your bath for school tomorrow." No. It was, "Do you want to come in now and have your bath?" This is what I meant. This wouldn't stop the playing for them, so I would have to go outside. It seemed to be my job to be the one to spoil their fun. Carla asked her father once why he never gave them a curfew like their mother. His reply was, "I think you'll come home when you're good and ready": words of wisdom from her Daddy showing kindness to his children. You can guess these words didn't sit well with their mother.

Carl enjoyed doing things with his girls, going on adventures in the bush with them, their little legs practically running to keep up to their Daddy's long strides. He was used to this walking-in-the-bush thing and it was as if he was almost running, like he didn't know how to slow down, even for a little bit. This was one of his favourite places to be and he taught them about nature on these outings, pointing out the natural beauty of the wildflowers growing unobstructed along the trails. They also learned about the different animal tracks and their leftovers that were found on the ground along the way that could tell us which one had crossed the path before us.

After a fun day, we would head home with the girls clutching their favourite wildflowers in their hands. When we arrived home, the flowers would be put in a jar of fresh water to be enjoyed and admired for days to come.

———— ∽∾⦵⧼⧽∾∽ ————

While the girls were still quite young, Carl decided he had had his fill of working in the red dust, even though it was what the town of Atikokan was built on. This was September 9, 1973. He started work the following day on September 10, 1973 for the Great Lakes Paper Company. This new company had its headquarters in Thunder Bay, and this was to be the first day of operations in their new bush camp at

Brule Creek in the Huronian area. This camp was about a forty-five-minute drive east of Atikokan.

Carl had the job of driving the man-haul bus, which was a school bus used to pick up the workers and take them to the jobsite and then back home at the end of the workday. He would then check the oil and other things under the hood, making sure it was road worthy for the following day. He also swept out the bus and cleaned it for the men, sometimes wiping down the seats, scrubbing the floor, and cleaning the windows. Yes, he took care of the bus like it was one of his cars. He was to work in this area until its closure after he had put twenty-three years of his blood and sweat into this job.

From here he went to Ignace where he worked for the same company until he retired. At this new job he worked hard but was happier, doing what he liked out in the forest. He operated many different machines over the course of the years. He was a skidder operator at one point: skidding the cut trees to the roadside where they were to be loaded onto pulp trucks and delivered to the mill in Thunder Bay. He was also a slasher operator; a slasher was a machine that picked up the trees and cut them into eight-foot lengths, stacking them into neat piles. He was also a harvester operator or feller buncher operator. (A feller buncher was a large machine which cut the trees down and piled them into bundles for the grapple to take out to the roadside.) He also had his share of operating the grader, keeping the roads levelled so the trucks could get in to pick up the wood.

The one job that Carl wasn't particularly fond of was operating the fuel truck, going around and fuelling up the machines so they would be ready to go for another day. With this job, getting fuel on your clothes was not something you wanted to happen. The smell of the fuel would stay with you until you returned home for a shower and change of clothes. The company eventually brought a new machine into the bush. It was a large machine called a "chipper" that chipped the trees up into wood chips which were then loaded into "chip trucks" and hauled to the Thunder Bay Mill for processing.

There were times when Carl was used by the company to train the younger workers on the safe operating of the different machines. He would be proud to have this honour and would teach them well, passing on his skills much like the job of teaching his daughters to drive when the time came for them to get their licenses.

During the course of his work years, he suffered more than a few injuries: cutting his leg with the axe, chipping the bone in his heel when a tree jumped back, and injuring the muscle in his shoulder which left him unable to lift his arm beyond the height of his elbow. As well, Carl suffered from rheumatoid arthritis which caused him lots of pain in his hands and wrists.

The biggest injury to happen to him was the loss of two fingers and broken bones in his hand the night he caught his hand in the saw blade of his machine. At that time, if memory serves me right, this was not a regular machine of the company, for some reason. This particular machine had a piece cut out of the guard which covers the blade for safety reasons. This truly would never pass a safety check with the standards in place to protect the workers today.

There was no middle finger after this loss, or ring finger for that matter. They both ended up in the bush that night, gone, never to be seen again. Maybe his pet fox buried them and had a small service with the other animals that Carl had befriended in his daily working adventures. Maybe it was a thank-you for showing them kindness—and for all the picnic lunches he had provided for them.

It took seven months for Carl to heal up enough to return to work, after getting just plain worn out and tired of being harassed by the Worker's Compensation Board. They are supposed to be there to support the injured workers, however in Carl's case, I didn't see much support. Rather, they seemed to want him back to work as soon as possible, come hell or high water, whether he was ready to return or not.

He went back without his doctor's okay, with one stitch still remaining in his hand—they couldn't get it out. He didn't like the constant frustration of dealing with those above him, and I think he had suffered enough. After losing these two digits, there was lots of frustrated attempts at trying to button up a shirt. Another was simply trying to drink a cup of coffee, which caused many spills. There was a great loss of strength in his hand which was another setback that was annoying. And, no, the fingers wouldn't be growing back anytime soon.

If I'm allowed my two cents worth or opinion on this tragedy, it would be this: *no man should have to work in the bush at night to begin with!* Having only owls for company! And, of course, with other creatures peering at you in the dark! The possibilities of bad things happening are endless! Where is the common sense in that?

Later on, during a trip to Carl's doctor in Thunder Bay, we spotted the machine parked beside the highway...burnt! Sitting there all charred and black? Was this an omen? No one else would be getting hurt on it again!

Life was good working in the bush—all was well in the forest. He enjoyed the wildlife he encountered during his years, especially his pet fox. A moose that tried to climb into the doorway of the bus one night caused quite a lot of excitement! One night he came across a pygmy owl perched in a tree watching him work. With the reflection of the lights from his machine, he enjoyed watching this little creature swivelling his head around, almost in a complete circle. Times had certainly changed for Carl from the days of working on the tractor when living on the farm, sitting on a wooden milk crate, with his cap perched safely on his head.

During the course of working in the woodlands, safety was to be a major concern for the company. Keeping the men safe on the job also meant keeping the Workers' Compensation costs down. There were to be lots of safety meetings held for the workers where the company couldn't stress this fact enough. After working so long without an injury, the company would reward them with a safety banquet where they would receive gifts for their achievements. They also preached that safety began in the home. During one meeting, Carl stood and made a comment on this fact, stating that the wives should then be invited to their suppers. They were instrumental in sending their men off to work in a happy frame of mind. To him this made good sense. From then on, after this eye-opener, the wives no longer spent the evening at home without their loved ones but joined them on their special night out. Thank you, Carl, for being instrumental in having the ladies included in your night of celebration.

Over the years, the Great Lakes Paper Company was to change hands a few times: Canadian Pacific Forest Products, Avenor, and eventually Bowater, where Carl was to retire after his twenty-nine years of working. Due to the fact that he had started on the first day of operation, he was high on the seniority list which allowed him a few opportunities when it came to job postings, vacation time, and other job perks.

At this time, we sold our small house on Black Road and bought a larger one on Abbott Road, the street we had lived on when we started out as newlyweds. Our new address was 215 Abbott Road, and the move was made in August 1979. This home was a new build and came with three bedrooms, a large kitchen, dining room combined, living room, and also a mud room. It was built on a full-size poured basement, and the lot size was the biggest on the street, unless you were lucky and had two lots.

The girls were happy living here, each having their own bedroom, a nice change for sure. They enjoyed their time spent with their father while growing up and had a few adventures along the way. While mother was at work, you just never knew what the plans might be. Maybe some fun on the new three-wheeler.

This, on one occasion, ended up with Corina going for a swim in May. When Carl picked Carla and I up from a work-related meeting, he casually mentioned that Corina had been in swimming that day, like they had planned it that way. Much to my shock in hearing this news, I remarked that it was too early for swimming; the water wouldn't have been warm enough yet. I soon found out that it was a small mishap with the three-wheeler and not planned the way it turned out. One of her special friends was driving and Corina was a passenger when they ended up in the lake. The result was the girls getting a quick bath. Being the machine was still running, it made its way across the lake where they were able to retrieve it. All turned out well in the end.

Corina was to have another learning experience on this machine after putting it through the skirting on the home of one of our neighbours who lived behind us. No injuries, but the lady of the house was quite upset. She was a bit on the wild side after this error in judgment. Carl was quick to make the necessary repairs, leaving the skirting in better shape than it was before the impact of the three-wheeler.

Another incident that unnerved me was another occasion when this machine was involved; this time the driver was Carla. Her father took off on a run with her as a passenger. After hearing something, I looked out the window and, lo and behold, there she came down the street towing a large tree behind her. Her father...nowhere to be seen! He had let her bring home this tree for a clothesline pole, all alone on the three-wheeler and sharing the road with vehicular traffic!

Sometimes I would shake my head in amazement at what he trusted his young girls to do. More than likely it was similar to the way he had been raised with his parents trusting him with responsibilities and letting him make his own path in life. He never had gray hair, likely because he didn't worry about the small things. Not at all like me!

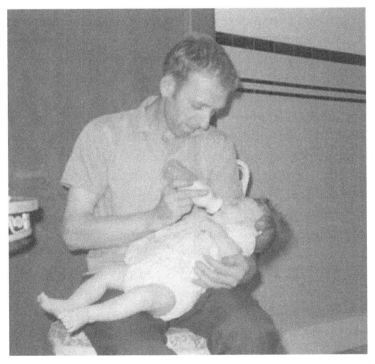

Carl looking after Carla while I tree planted. 110 McKenzie Ave West.

Our first home on 101 Black Road, Pink and Cherry. Corina in flower bed.

Carl showing off the kitchen cupboards that he built.

Carl and Corina enjoying themselves at a wedding dance.

Carl and the girls camping in Duluth Mn.

Carla, Corina and Carl at the Valley Fair.

Carl's favourite place to be – in the fresh air, enjoying
nature with the scent of pine trees in the air.

Carl on the way to pick up the men with the man-
haul bus, then off to work at Huronian.

TRAINING CERTIFICATE

HAVING SUCCESSFULLY COMPLETED
A COURSE OF INSTRUCTION,

CARL BOLEN

IS AWARDED THIS CERTIFICATE IN RECOGNITION OF HIS
PROFICIENCY AS A

BUS DRIVER

Dated at Thunder Bay, Ontario, this 30. day of July, 19 75

MANAGER OF WOODLANDS   TRAINING CO-ORDINATOR

An important piece of paper for his wallet.

Celebrating our 25th Wedding Anniversary Sept 17, 1990.

Waltzing across Texas with Ernest Tubb.

Corina standing at the Bolen Road sign in Shenston.

Carl dancing father of the bride dance with his girl Carla.

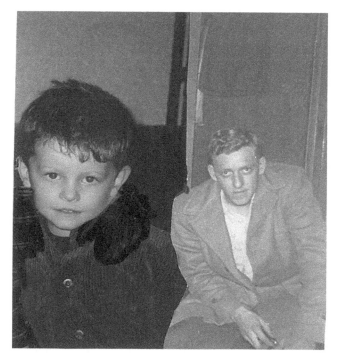

My two "look-alikes" Keighan and his grandpa.

Naptime for grandpa and Graesen.

That captivating smile that had me from day one!

Christmas in Thunder Bay – Grandma, Kharis,
Graesen, Keighan and Grandpa.

Kharis spending time with Grandpa.

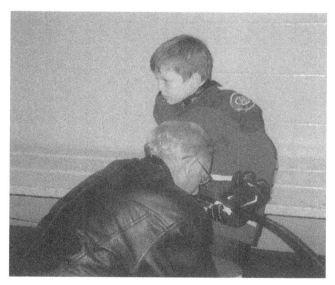

Grandpa helping Keighan with his skates.

Grandpa and Jaycelin making snowmen.

Grandpa and Jaycelin – reading after she was discharged
from hospital following surgery on her tummy.

CHAPTER NINE

Friendships and Flurries

One of the neighbourhood families that Carl and I grew fond of over the years was the Lemieux family: Pat and Bernice along with their children Austin, Patrick, Galen, and Kitty. We got to know them quite well as their next-door neighbours when we lived in our house on McKenzie Avenue at the beginning of our journey together. This was at the early stages of our married life, having moved there in 1966. Bernice was my crew boss when I was involved with the tree planting "episode." I say that because of the black flies tormenting me to the limit of my sanity. Also, Pat, her husband, worked with Carl in the Woodlands at Brule Creek in the Huronian District.

I helped Bernice out by "child sitting" her "animals" as she fondly called them back then. My job was to get them off to school in one piece. (Sorry boys! But sometimes I wondered if it was a losing battle.) This is when I was to learn that, yes, that old saying of "boys will be boys" was the spoken truth. Not only that but being in charge of children that were taller than me caused me to live in fear that this could be a problem.

Getting back to a more serious note, we were to make lasting friendships with the family. And now that their parents are both gone, we still keep a special bond with the children. Pat, or "little one" as his Mom called him, also had the nickname "Mooch," which is what he still goes by today. During his growing up days he was famous for his disappearing act, and we found ourselves looking for him more than a few times. He had a habit of going somewhere and not letting anyone know—like the time he rode his bicycle to Sapawe. I have to say he was the colourful one, always smiling and leaving smiles on the faces of others. And, I have to mention, he was good at "jeopardy" also. Galen was the tall, stately brother who manned the stove in the mornings all those years ago. He was very good at frying perfect eggs for breakfast. There was to be no cereal for these growing boys.

In between the odd wrestling match and a good breakfast, they were on the way out the door to school. After his mother passed away, Galen took over the caregiving of his father, Pat, who at this time was in failing health and on oxygen. He had a special bond with his father, and was his "private" homecare worker, helping him with his daily needs, even trimming his hair when it was needed. Pat trusted his boy with his care and didn't complain.

The Lemieux family also enjoyed playing sports, namely baseball. They never missed a game, regardless if the playing field was on the muddy side after a rain or if they were being eaten alive by mosquitoes that thrived with the river close by. Bernice never missed a game, cheering on her children. They still play today, and I would bet Bernice is still keeping her eye on them from above.

Kitty was the youngest of the family, stepping in to fill her mother's shoes after her passing. Cooking and cleaning, keeping the holiday spirit alive, with help of course from the boys, was now her goal. The Lemieux home was famous for its decorations on the front lawn at Hallowe'en and Christmas. I think everyone who could would drive past to check it out, not wanting to miss seeing this spectacular display. Kitty would also give her mom and dad two grandsons: Galen known as "little" Galen, and a second boy, Gary. These were blessings for Pat and Bernice to love and spoil, and that they did.

Both of these boys were raised with a loving touch and grew up to be kind and considerate members of our neighbourhood. They would help when you needed help. Gary, I remember, gave me a ride to the emergency department when I couldn't drive myself. Little Galen and his mom planted a cherry tree for me after Carl had passed away. Yes, the family was always there if you needed help. Also, Kitty was my main "sitter" in the years when my girls were young.

Austin was to leave Atikokan and he lives out West. He still plays the guitar and sings, just like his mother did before him. The Lemieux family will always remain dear to my heart. If I need a friend, I know I can always count on them.

Another family I can't forget that Carl and I also grew fond of were the Sportak family. They lived down the street from us on Abbott Road: Bill and Diane and their children, Sandra, Roy, Sharon, Gary, and Ruth. There were always sleepovers, birthday parties, and other things that would get them together.

Speaking of other things, Ruth was the one operating the three-wheeler when Corina went for a swim that day. Ruth was devastated, and probably still is to this day. I wonder if Carl got excited. I don't think so; it takes a lot to ruffle his feathers. I trust Ruth has put this behind her. We learn as we go, usually from something we least expect. If you were to ask Carl, he would agree, saying once that he lost track of how many times he had fallen down. A person has to start somewhere with this learning thing. Ruth's just started out a bit different—learning to drive and having a quick swim at the same time. Gary was to retrieve the three-wheeler after it made its way across the lake, so there was no harm done.

The Sportak family were to take Corina and Carla "under their wing" while I was still working at Cherie's Café. I never had to worry if it got busy and I was late getting off work, knowing that the girls were being cared for.

Mr. Sportak was in ill health, suffering from a hereditary kidney disease which was slowly creeping through his family. He was put on the transplant list, and after receiving a donor kidney, he was to lose it later because it failed. He was set up with home dialysis, which was to save him the trouble of having to journey to Thunder Bay three times a week. He was a kind man even with all of his suffering and was also very proud of his children. He taught them to grow up to be responsible young men and women. He was also fortunate, like Carl, to have his own private nurse. Sandra assisted him with his daily needs, especially when put on home dialysis.

On quite a few occasions we were invited by the Sportak family to take part in their Christmas Eve dinner. This was a big event, with all the Ukrainian specialities that Bill enjoyed. His wife, Diane, and their daughters would spend the day cooking and getting ready for this special feast. One thing I remember when going to the Sportak home was always being treated like royalty. After our Christmas feast, we would make our way home and the Sportak family would be off to attend Midnight Mass at their church.

One Christmas Eve, Roy poured Carl a "toast" of Christmas cheer. To make a long story short, Carl, not being used to this beverage, found out when he stood up to leave that his legs didn't want to cooperate with his plan of walking to the car. Roy was quick to help him get safely seated and ready for the ride home. His hair was to get mussed during this "move," and Roy lovingly called him "Alf," a nickname that stuck with him for quite some time.

After arriving home and getting Carl settled for the night, it was Santa time. No Mr. Santa this year. It was to be Mrs. Santa taking that chore on; meanwhile Santa was sound asleep. The next day we were to head west to Stratton for the chance to spend some time with our family. A knock came on the door and Roy was standing on the step. His father had sent him down to our house to drive us to Stratton. This was to make amends for the Christmas cheer episode from the night before. Yes, Mr. "B" as they called him, or "Alf," after having his hair stand on end the night before, was to make a full recovery and we set off for Stratton a bit late, but on the road nevertheless.

This is a fond memory of Roy that was dear to our hearts. Another was when he borrowed Carl's axe for a project he was working on at home. While using it, he accidently broke the handle off the axe. Rather than tell his father, he brought the axe back to Carl to see if he could fix it. His dad was to never know of this event—Carl fixed the axe as good as new. Once more, all was good in the forest. The way Roy handled this is another example of Mr. Sportak teaching his children to be responsible citizens during their growing up days.

Mr. Sportak was to pass away after years of ill health and a few years later his wife, Diane, also passed away. They were both still young. I wish them many blessings. They raised their family and taught them well.

Today Roy, as well as his sister Sharon, who both live in Thunder Bay, are undergoing dialysis from the results of having the same disease that their father had. Sandra had been a kidney donor for Sharon, however the kidney was later lost after an illness, I believe. There is a great need for organ donors. If you are able to sign a donor card, please do so. You could save a life, maybe even a friend. When the Kidney Foundation comes calling, please be generous; help find a cure.

Sending you lots of strength and prayers, Roy and Sharon. Stay strong, and don't lose your sense of humour, Roy!

———————

I had a close girlfriend, Karen Advent, who had made plans with me to go to the Marvel School of Hairdressing after we completed high school. We had been good friends all through our school years when we attended Patullo #8, a one room country school. We had many memories of those years and both of us continued on to the high school together in Rainy River.

I never got to go to Winnipeg with Karen as my mother had serious heart problems at the time. She couldn't look after the younger children, or herself for that matter. My sister and I took turns staying home from school to help out and both of us ended up quitting school when we started getting behind with our lessons. This ended my dream of getting my Grade 12 diploma and setting off to Winnipeg with Karen and making our hairdressing dreams come true.

Karen went off to Winnipeg and made a future for herself doing what she had planned, which makes me happy. She still lives in Winnipeg and is now retired.

On the other hand, I fared well: Carl and I got married. Maybe he plotted this, getting the ring out of the glove box before I could get away on him. Distance is hard on the heart, remembering the letters from the bunkhouse days. After moving to Atikokan, I got my Grade 12 diploma, taking part in the Adult Education Program through the high school. I was rather proud of my marks, most of them in the nineties. So, now I don't call myself a high school dropout anymore.

Then again, I didn't miss out on the hairdressing experience, not totally anyway, cutting Carl's hair and my own during our married life. I enjoyed this special time I spent cutting and styling Carl's hair. We shared some good conversation and the haircuts turned out top notch, if I do say so myself! After I was finished, I would shake the loose hair outside over our deck rail and vacuum while he went to the powder room to check his hair in the mirror and adjust his curls on his forehead. All in all, I think things turned out for the best; maybe a little nick here and there with the clippers, usually around the ears, but nothing too serious.

Karen and I used to correspond with each other when we worked in the Nestor Falls area, back when phoning wasn't as convenient as it is today. She was always bubbly and happy, and we shared many laughs over the course of our friendship. In one of her letters, she asked how Carl was doing and if I was keeping him in his stall. I would have to be honest and say, "Of course I wasn't." He had this tendency to kick loose and head out to the pasture for a good run, much like my father's horses. Yes, it wasn't easy to keep him confined in one place for sure. He enjoyed the freedom of the highway, the fresh air on his face. And, living life his way...what else can you think of for a young man? Enjoy being alive! I say, you only pass this way once, so you'd best keep that in mind!

———— ⁓⁓⚬⚬✛⚬⚬⁓⁓ ————

Living on McKenzie Avenue gave me a new lease on life. It was only one block from Main Street, and this got me out into the public more. And being that I didn't have my licence to drive yet, I no longer lived such a sheltered life as I did on the farm when I lived eight miles from the Village of Stratton.

It wasn't long before I was hired as a tree planter which got me out into the forest, my favourite place to be as well as Carl's. This job meant catching a bus downtown at six o'clock in the morning which took us to our planting site. This work was to replace trees that had previously been harvested by men making a living. The work itself wasn't easy; you had a quota to plant and if the terrain was rough, it could do a number on your body. By the end of your shift you started to feel the weariness creeping in.

This job was another partnership for Carl and me. He cut the trees down, and I replaced them. I enjoyed this work, especially when I would come across a patch of lady slippers that were prone to blossom in the spring. They were surely a picture of beauty in the forest, miles from civilization, and I have to say they are still my favourite along with wild roses and violets. May flowers were in abundance also, growing and enjoying the cover of the forest, adding their touch of beauty.

There was a new annoyance in the Atikokan wilds—swarms of black flies attacking you for a taste of your blood. They were out in full force in the dampness of the springtime and were mean little buggers. We were very fortunate not to have them in Stratton is all I can say. They were sort of like the moose I guess, needing the muskeg to survive. They didn't pick favourites when they were hungry, which seemed to be all the time.

These new little creatures and I didn't get along very well, with me being allergic to their bites, sometimes having both of my eyes swollen shut at the same time. A trip to Thunder Bay after having blood poisoning twice from them was to be an end to my tree planting days. After finally being tested later in life, the allergy specialist told my daughter that I could die from them—much the same as a bee sting for some people.

———〰〰〰〰〰———

Back to an earlier topic, my daughters told me much later that they just never knew what their Dad may have planned for the day after I was safely out of the house at work. This was a perfect time for him to crank up the country tunes and get busy with something. One day I arrived home to find that he had the wild idea to make homemade root beer. I now know that it was one of his favourite drinks with cream soda being his absolute favourite. He didn't just make a small batch; no, he had to go whole hog and make lots, running out of containers to put it in. Even the large mixing bowl I used for making bread was full.

I have no idea how he planned to keep this in a safe, drinkable state, being there was no way he could possibly store such a large amount in the fridge. I'm still not sure where he bought the mix, but I do remember it came in a bottle. The girls recall him having to run to the store to buy more sugar after having run out. They enjoyed watching their father scurrying around the kitchen, up to his mischievous stuff. They were probably full to their ears with root beer by the time I got home from work.

Another fun event that that took place in the kitchen at Easter was making their dad's "flamingo eggs." This was his special recipe for pickled eggs which he made with the girls, putting the eggs in jars and dying them different colours like Easter eggs. This became a tradition in the years to come.

With his love for country music, another fun thing was making cassette tapes with his favourite songs. One had to be extra quiet when this was going on as he used one machine to tape off the other machine, skipping the songs that were not his favourites. It was time-consuming work, with him having to figure out how much room was left on the blank tape and which song would fit that space. On one of his tapes, I could hear our little dog barking; on another I heard a door opening and closing.

The girls smile today thinking of their father and his zest for life. He was proud of his girls, his pride and joy. Being the youngest in his family, he wasn't used to having little ones to keep track of, but he seemed to do a good job raising them.

He didn't get rattled very easy either, but I can recall one incident when they were chasing each other around the house and Carl was napping on the chesterfield. Did you ever notice if something is going to happen it's usually when someone is having a nap? It seemed to be that way at our house that day. This time, a rubber eraser was being used which they were throwing at each other. One let the eraser fly and accidently hit their father between the eyes, which caused him to come to life quite abruptly. It all ended well, and Carl was soon back to his nap. If I recall correctly, it wasn't the first time he was jarred from a sound sleep. Gosh, a man can't seem to get any rest.

Another incident he was annoyed by, which was a bit more serious, happened when I was working at "Cherie's Café" which just happened to be the busiest place in town at that time. He had driven downtown to pick me up at work, and I kindly asked him if he would put my garbage outside in the bin for me. This was out back of the café and of course it was quite dark back there. He let the first bag fly and, unbeknown to him, just at that moment the skunk inside came alive, glad to finally get a chance to use what nature equipped it with to get rid of annoyances like my sweet little man. Carl, instantly madder than a proverbial wet hen and dripping with skunk juice, proceeded to throw the rest of the bags in. The atmosphere in the car on the drive home was dangerously tense, also heavy with the smell of skunk in the air. The windows on the car were frozen up and we couldn't get fresh air in to help the situation. It also didn't take too much common sense to know someone in the car wasn't very happy. This friendly skunk must have had a home under the garbage shed and had come out of hibernation for a snack to take the chill off.

After a long shower, Carl settled himself down; but I did notice it took quite a while for the skunk odour to disappear from the car. He became a proud owner of a new wallet and leather belt. His others had to be thrown out. Skunks have a tendency to come out from their winter sleep when you least expect it, much like a squirrel who will also make an appearance off and on over the course of that long winter nap.

Getting past this skunk episode, something fun Carl enjoyed was taking the girls camping. He went on a shopping spree and got everything we needed for our camping trips. To start with, we enjoyed camping with a tent. Then we bought a tent trailer which had a stove, fridge, sink, table, and places to sleep. What more could you want? We started out camping at Trowbridge Falls, venturing to Duluth, and finally on to Minneapolis.

The trip to Minneapolis was to be an adventure before we arrived there. Carl had fastened a luggage carrier to the roof of our car, but something went wrong and we lost Carla's suitcase on the highway outside the city. Not a good spot for recovery with all of the traffic flying past. By the time we retraced our steps to where it had come off, there was nothing left! Someone must have scooped up all her belongings, leaving her with only what she was wearing. The sad thing was the suitcase was full of her school clothes that we had just purchased.

After getting into the city, Carl proceeded to find himself very lost, ending up going through the same tunnel four times which had a sign at the entrance saying, "No Explosives." I wasn't sure if that meant propane tanks or not, but I kept myself quiet about it, which was a chore. One of the things I had learned was to keep quiet and not say anything; he'll find his way out eventually. Which we did! Not to the campground we were planning on staying at, but a campground. We stayed put here until it was time to pack up and head on out of there.

While camping, Carl enjoyed doing all the cooking—his breakfasts were the best, our favourite of the day, with his fried potatoes, bacon, eggs, and of course camp toast to top it off. He left us many happy memories to think about in days to come.

CHAPTER TEN

Life After the Hardhat

When Carl was in his late fifties, not wanting to give up working yet, his job started to wind down at Huronian. The only thing left out there in the line of a paycheque was cutting brush with a saw strapped to your waist. Unfortunately, this wasn't a job he liked; especially having fallen down a few times. If my guess is on track, maybe the saw was weighing him down causing the falls. He decided it was time to move to Ignace to do his usual work for the same company which had a camp there. In Ignace, he rented an apartment which he shared with another worker, Lloyd Haney from Atikokan, and the two of them would make the trip home on their days off.

He would bring a grocery list with him of supplies to take back to keep him cooking in the days following. Most times he would only come home every two weeks. In the meantime, he would walk downtown and phone me from a payphone. Yes, this life was sort of like our life before we were married—only it was now phoning instead of letter writing.

Carl didn't have a second vehicle, so he travelled back and forth with Lloyd. Sometimes Carl would do the driving. They shared expenses of having the apartment and each of them did their own cooking. There were other friends from their working days at Huronian who had made the switch to Ignace as well. Maurice Chabot was one, another was Marty Ranta, as well as others from their earlier years. Being Carl didn't have transportation, Marty would pick him up at his apartment and take him out for coffee. Carl enjoyed these outings and mentioned them often, having the highest regard for Marty. He also spoke often of Maurice over the following years.

Carl continued working in Ignace until his retirement on November 29, 2002—his sixty-fifth birthday. He had worked for this company since September 10, 1973, which gave him over twenty-nine years on the job. Yes, lots of miles were put on his work boots, some of them not easy. To be honest, I was a bit disappointed at the send-off he was given: nothing special, just a regular day of work. Blood, sweat and tears, that's how I call it: working hard in the woodlands, earning his paycheques honestly. I wasn't sure if the head honchos in the office even realized that he was gone. His working days were over.

A couple of months later he was to receive a past due notice in the mail regarding his union dues. After calling the union's head office in Thunder Bay and informing them of his retirement, which was a surprise to them it seemed, he was to receive some very nice framed documents and congratulations from them.

Much later, the company he worked for called him from Thunder Bay and asked him if he would drive there to pick up his retirement gift and have his picture taken. I wonder where they were when the bus pulled into the drop off point on his last shift? Giving the gift then would have made better sense to me. If I may be allowed to tell the truth, it wasn't worth the trip driving a good four hours to pick it up. Yes, it ended up being a ski jacket that appeared to weigh more than him. I believe it had elastic around the waist and was almost knee length. It came with a long black scarf to top it off. I'm left wondering how many men who spent the better part of their lives working in the bush would love to have one of these! Carl had never skied in the course of his lifetime and just wasn't ready to start now at his age. It reminded me of other awards that he received for safety: a few extra-large sweatshirts had made their way into his hands, which he was unable to wear. If you were to take a close look at Carl, you would know that size small would be more suitable.

There, that's off my chest now. Hopefully a lesson will be learned here. I tend to straighten things out for Carl (taking the apron off as I like to call it), his being a quiet man and not one to make a fuss. You will find evidence of my sorting things out here and there as I go.

His girls finished up their school days in Atikokan with Carla leaving first after graduation from Grade 12 to attend nurse's training at Confederation College in Thunder Bay.

Corina followed later, and after trying her hand at different options, she ended up going the distance to become a teacher. On her way to this accomplishment, she also graduated from being a dental assistant, plus receiving the Dean's Medal in Early Childhood Education. For a time, I thought maybe she just might continue on going to college and university, never mind stopping and going out to work.

Carl was the proud father of a Registered Nurse, which was to be a blessing in the years to come when his health started to fail. She was to get her first nursing job at McKellar Hospital in Thunder Bay, working on the pediatric ward. This job was to last almost ten years until they started to scale back with a huge lay off, which eventually led to the closure of this hospital.

From here she changed directions and began her journey working for dental surgeons, putting her nursing skills to good use: administering IV sedation to patients having surgery in the office and monitoring their recovery until they were able to be discharged. She is still working in this field at the present time, a career that she enjoys and is happy at.

Meanwhile Corina is busy teaching school at the North Star School in Atikokan, currently teaching the Grade 1 class. She enjoys this group of children and makes learning fun for them.

Now with both girls settled into their chosen professions, time had certainly changed direction for him, going from a young boy growing up on the farm to this milestone: a whole new chapter in this life. And one that he was proud to have experienced.

Carla was to meet her soulmate, Dean, in Thunder Bay while he was there from Manitoba working on a job. After a courtship and engagement, they set their wedding date. It was to be held in Montego Bay, Jamaica, a beautiful place to make your promises and say your "I do's."

She and her husband blessed us with three children in the coming years: first came Graesen, who was born on my birthday, just like I might have planned it. Next in line came Keighan, followed by Kharis. Carl was the proudest of grandfathers, spoiling them all.

Corina also blessed us with a daughter, Jaycelin, whom Carl took an active role in raising and was to keep a close eye on in the coming years. They lived with us for a period of time before getting situated into their new home on Larson Street, a block and a bit away from our home.

Carl enjoyed attending their special events and spent much time with them in their younger days. He enjoyed hanging out with the two boys, which was to be a new experience for him. He spent lots of time out playing in the backyard with them doing "boy things." Golfing with their plastic golf clubs and balls was one of the pastimes they enjoyed.

Going on walks with Grandpa was another favourite, especially if it took them to Minnow Pond just west of our house and up a steep hill towards the airport. There were lots of minnows to catch here, and what boy doesn't enjoy this fun? They would take empty margarine containers to put their "catch" in. The girls were also involved in Grandpa's treks, enjoying the wildflowers along the trails. Gathering pinecones and bringing them home to make crafts—which was to be another fun time. An odd trip down Highway 622 to see if the fish were biting was another good way to spend an afternoon.

I can't recall bringing a fish home with us, but the grandchildren enjoyed this sport and wanted to fish as often as possible. Going out to Little Falls and trying to get a bite was also fun…if you escaped alive after the onslaught of mosquitoes looking for a feast.

Another trip worth mentioning was going out to the blueberry patch. The kids enjoyed getting out into the bush, and after picking berries until they grew bored, would spend their time playing and running around, once actually trying to catch a moose! On all of our outings we always had a packed picnic lunch to enjoy.

Swimming at French Lake and Crystal Lake beach was a summer event that we would definitely have to squeeze into our plans. On those hot summer days, the grandkids wouldn't let us forget about this. Grandpa enjoyed watching them swim and having fun in the water.

Getting back to the blueberry patch for a minute, I must say Graesen and Keighan were to get lots of practice driving on the back roads getting set to go for their driver's licences. Yes, they put quite a few miles on and were ready for their driving lessons in the city to begin.

Attending live hockey games was something else our two grandsons brought into our lives. A lively game, we both enjoyed cheering them on, especially when one of them would shoot the puck into the net and score a goal. This game was to keep us busy as each boy played on a different team, meaning there would be many games to take in. Carl's last hockey game was in his transport chair bundled up with blankets to keep him warm as now he had lost the ability to walk safely. It was nice to take him to a game of Keighan's before he was bedridden. This game was held at the Fort William Gardens.

Keighan still plays hockey for the Thunder Bay North Stars and Graesen plays for the Fighting Walleye. Graesen also had a love of playing football for Hammarskjold High School and proved to be quite good at it. Kharis was on the cheerleading team, busy cheering on the boys, something she enjoyed with others from her high school. Over the years she had the privilege of attending many hockey games, supporting her brothers in a game they both loved.

Jaycelin enjoyed being active as well with figure skating in her early years then on to skiing and running. She is not afraid to get up early and go for a morning run to start her day.

Family back row: Corina Bolen, Dean Gerrie, Carla Gerrie, Carl Bolen, Centre Row: Graesen and Keighan Gerrie (grandsons), Front row: Gramma Farmer (Violet Schram), Valerie Bolen. To the left Jaycelin Bolen, to the right centre, Kharis Gerrie, (granddaughters).

Grandpa Carl with hockey players: Left, Graesen, Right Keighan Gerrie, Granddaughters, Kharis Gerrie, Jaycelin Bolen.

A new friend surprised Carl with a visit at Crystal Beach.

Jaycelin playing tricks on her grandpa.

Blueberry picking at Sunshine on the Bending Lake Road with Jaycelin.

——⟿⦵⟋⦵⦵⟋⦵⦵⟍⟍⟋⟍⟍⟋⦵⟍⟿——

When Grandpa Carl retired, he had more time to spend with his grandchildren, just like his grandpa before him. He would take the boys for walks looking for fossils, a favourite of Graesen's, which usually meant searching for pretty rocks. Another chore he enjoyed was helping the boys put on their skates and tying them up for them. With the appearance of the girls, Kharis and Jaycelin, the activities changed a bit. Sometimes he would be sporting a new hairdo, wearing a few barrettes or maybe a small ponytail. Yes, he kept his grandchildren busy doing crafts, puzzles, lots of colouring, and reading many a bedtime story.

Jaycelin and her Mom, having spent time living with us before their move, were to keep Grandpa busy and out of mischief. He accompanied his young charge to play group when she was still too young to attend school. Also, Grandpa took care of her during the day while her Mom was at work.

One day when I arrived home from my work at the hospital, I was to find the two of them trying to mop up a major flood in the kitchen. Actually, Jaycelin was sliding in her bare feet and Grandpa was standing in ankle deep water with his leather slippers on. Even the kitchen cupboards were full of water caused because of a drawer left open. I guess Carl was planning on doing dishes and in the meantime got busy with Jaycelin working on a project, completely forgetting that he had left the tap on. This was brought to his attention when Jaycelin heard water running. It took quite a while to get the kitchen back in order, as you can imagine.

Jaycelin thought it was lots of fun and had many fond memories of Grandpa. She still remembers the walks they went on and commented that Grandpa's pockets would be filled with pretty rocks when they arrived back home. They also picked many pinecones, sometimes painting them and gluing sparkles on them.

I have to mention the hatching out parties at the North Star School as well. When Jaycelin finally started her schooling, Grandpa was always there for special occasions, especially the "Hatching Out Party" when the baby chicks would hatch out of the eggs. Each of the classrooms had plugged in incubators which had lights to keep the eggs warm, enabling them to hatch. This took the place of the mother hen who would normally be sitting on the eggs, turning them daily to help the hatching process along. The classroom teacher would take on this responsibility and keep a close eye on the eggs when it was time for the baby chicks to make their way out of the shell. This was an exciting event for the students when the hatching out party was happening. It attracted lots of town folk who came to enjoy having a first-hand look at the little chicks. There were other fun things going on at this event as well along with a BBQ with hotdogs for everyone. Carl never missed this event and enjoyed having Jaycelin take him around the school to show him her classroom and what she had been doing for schoolwork. The North Star School was a place for having fun while learning at the same time.

Another event that caused lots of excitement was the Christmas concert when Jaycelin would wait patiently for Grandpa's arrival. She looked forward to having him there to watch her perform on the stage with her classmates and friends singing Christmas songs or maybe acting in a play. Yes, it was a magical time of the year and there was so much excitement among the children. Once again, she would proudly take him to her classroom and show him her schoolwork.

The Christmas concert was the end of school until after the holidays. You can imagine the happy students looking forward to the day when Santa Claus would make an appearance in the darkness of night. Just the thought of being a young child again, enjoying the magic of the season, was sure to be a lasting memory.

CHAPTER ELEVEN

The Battle Begins

It was concert time in December 2012 when our lives were to take a sudden turn. Corina and Jaycelin were waiting patiently for Grandpa Carl to show up. In the meantime, I was working my shift at the local hospital, so I was unable to attend, something I didn't like to miss. Having a job meant that I just couldn't take in everything no matter how much I wished I could. Grandpa was late, which caused Corina and Jaycelin much stress. Where could he be? No one was answering the telephone at home, so something wasn't quite right.

It turns out he was confused and lost his way to the North Star School after all the special functions he had attended there with Jaycelin. He ended up at the St. Patrick's School instead, not quite sure where he was at the time. The school called Corina and let her know that he was there, which proved to be devastating news for her and Jaycelin. They spent the afternoon in a state of sadness, knowing Grandpa was in big trouble this time, and if what they suspected was true, it would change our lives forever.

Driving used to be a source of pride for Carl from chauffeuring his siblings to and fro, along with the happy memories of driving the Lutheran ladies home from his mother's after a quilting session. He had been paid a quarter for this prestigious job, which put a smile on his face.

Some of his early driving was without a driver's licence, sitting on cushions to enable him to see over the dash and out the windshield. Later on, he was to drive himself to Rainy River for a valid driver's licence. After fibbing about his age, he left for home with one safely in his possession. Later, he would drive the manhaul bus when working for the Great Lakes Paper Company, always careful to return the workers home safely.

From the thrill of buying his first brand-new car at the tender age of eighteen to the purchase of many other cars in the years to come, the worst thing happened. This day of the Christmas concert was to be his last day of getting behind the wheel. He must have known deep down that it was over, as he never asked for the keys or even mentioned wanting to drive again. After all the years of enjoyment, it was time to call it a day. I always made sure he carried his driver's licence in his wallet even after the date had expired. Every once in a while he would take it out and examine it, which brought a smile to his face.

In the spring of 2013, after much testing, Carl was diagnosed with Alzheimer's disease. This was not going to end on a good note. In thinking back, I realized he was most likely fighting this for quite some time until he just couldn't hide it any longer. I was prone to blame much on his loss of hearing. One of his favourite things to say was, "Oh, I must have heard you wrong." He would say this after arriving home from the store with the wrong item, for instance pancake mix instead of flour when I was making bread. Or another example would be when he would do a quick run to the store for two items and return with only one, again, hearing me wrong.

Having worked at our local hospital in the dietary department for nearly seventeen years, I was exposed to this disturbing disease on a daily basis and was well aware of the outcome. The phases on its downhill spiral could be devastating, and there was only one way for this to end: down a rabbit hole, in the darkness, fighting for survival, not knowing where the twists and turns may take you.

To me, this disease was like a storm passing through in the night, with all its fury and destruction—not being able to see the damage until the following day when the sun was to come out once again. The damage, in this case, was the bits and pieces of Carl's brain that were beginning to disappear.

This left me with tears of despair running down my cheeks and vowing that I would care for him the best that I could in this, his time of need. He was my love, my best friend. We had planned on growing old together, and after spending the better part of our years together, our lives were about to change. I took on the challenge of caring for Carl at home where he would be happier, a place which held lots of memories for him.

———————

Along with the diagnosis of Alzheimer's soon came the need for pullups which he gracefully accepted, no questions asked. This transition was to take place after I discovered he had suffered from an accident. He didn't get to the little boy's room on time … to keep the dampness at bay he had literally stuffed paper towelling down his pants, using the entire roll. When I noticed his plight, he was visually remorseful and upset. After one of his showers, getting him into dry clothing, he was back to his happy *Old Spice* self. He never complained about the changes that were taking place and appreciated all my help when it came to being safe and secure.

It certainly doesn't do any harm to monitor their reactions to new medications they may be issued. Carl was put on a "miracle pill" to slow down the progression of this disease by his Alzheimer's specialist. He had an adverse reaction to the drug causing him to slur his words, to be in a zombie-like state, and to slobber! It was awful...not my idea of what I had in mind. After twelve days of showing no improvement, I stopped the medication. Some drugs may work for one but not necessarily for all. (For anyone caring for a loved one at home, retain your receipts relating to their care and take them with you when it is time to file your income tax. They can be claimed, providing a cash break for you in the end. In my case with Carl, I was required to get a prescription from his family doctor for proof of his needs.)

I must admit to the fact that my quiet, gentle man was prone to getting riled up on occasion. This is all part and parcel of this disease and can be quite stressful to the caregiver. Their memory can rapidly lose ground without warning. Suddenly they no longer recognize people including good friends and family members. Just seeing me speaking with a male family member caused Carl to become volatile, thinking

I had a new man in my life. This outburst was to shake me up to the depths of my soul.

After giving him some time and space, he calmed down and was back to himself in no time, forgetting what had just taken place. It may be difficult to do, but try not to take episodes like this personally because "they know not what they do."

Other than when I touched him with cold hands—which could cause a bit of a vocal outburst—the only other time he became riled was due to medication. This incident happened after his liver began to fail when his digestive system was unable to handle a new pill. After three days of taking the pill, he went into a distress mode, almost needing a straight jacket to settle him down. He was mean: kicking me, shaking me, hitting me, verbally abusing me, out of control. Fearing for his safety and mine as well, I managed to get him (after a battle) into his transfer chair, wearing only a pullup with his seatbelt on. Struggling, I managed to get him into the safety of our bedroom, covered up with a cozy blanket with the brakes on his chair activated. He would be less likely to harm himself this way.

Later on, after he calmed down, he slept for almost three days. The outcome of this fiasco for me was that I had a wound on the back of my hand that took more than a few days to heal. The result in my caring for Carl was to question medication combining—can they be safely mixed? I had done some research and discovered the pill was a narcotic and shouldn't have been mixed with what he was taking at the time. His liver failure didn't help matters, either. I learned to question medications for Carl, and I also found out what it means to be a spokesperson for someone who could not speak for himself.

These two happenings were major events for me to handle, when all "hell broke loose!" Other than that, we had a few quieter incidents I would like to forget. One was when he got out of control in a local restaurant for reasons unknown to me. This ended with him being disrespectful to the waitress who was serving our table and not deserving of the name he called her. I felt humiliated and remorseful, but all I could do was apologize for his behaviour and remove him from the scene.

Yes, life can be challenging for caregivers dealing with loved ones with Alzheimer's. But it's important to keep the love you have for them alive…suffer with them, keep them safe and never give up hope. It is all worth your while when you catch a glimpse of the rainbow after the storm has passed.

CHAPTER TWELVE

Dealing with the Devil

By this time, I had left my job at the hospital since it wasn't a good idea to leave Carl at home alone. One just never knew what he might have planned. Once I caught him with a cup of coffee sitting on the stove element with it turned on. He was planning on warming up his coffee. At the time I could visualize all sorts of things going wrong with this plan. Not good at all.

With the diagnosis of Alzheimer's, Carl was to end up with a doctor who specialized in this disease. We were to meet with her on occasion through the tele-health program where we would go to the hospital and have an appointment over the TV screen. Her best advice was to keep him comfortable, and knowing the prognosis of this affliction, there wasn't much out there to offer us hope on this new journey of Carl's.

During one of our meetings, she asked him to remove his shoes and socks and to then walk across the floor in his bare feet. After carefully watching him, she came to the conclusion that in two years' time he would most likely lose the ability to walk. This news was to cast a huge shadow over me that day. After all the walking Carl had enjoyed over the years, starting with his grandpa following him around keeping him safe, then going down the gravel road to visit friends, and finally, all the miles he put on his work boots trudging through the forest, to end up with this information was to cause us another hurdle to deal with.

We were set up at the hospital for a series of physiotherapy appointments to help him maintain his walking ability for as long as possible. We were to go twice a week, with Carl enjoying these outings. Getting out of his pajamas and dressed up in ordinary clothing was also a change for him.

After his sessions were over, I would take him on a cruise around town looking for deer. He enjoyed watching them foraging for food along the roadways, and after putting our vehicle in park, we would sit and enjoy observing them for a while. From here we would go for a coffee break, with Carl usually having a butter tart or a small fries and gravy—two of his favourites at the time. This was a nice way to get him out of the house and gave him a chance to meet some of his friends at the same time.

He also had many trips to Thunder Bay as well to meet up with his doctor. It was heartbreaking to say the least when her assistant would administer a quiz for him to complete. This enabled the doctor to tell how far along Carl was progressing with this debilitating disease. I recall one of the items on the test was to draw a clock, and then he was to put the numbers on the face. This was a challenge for him, and it was one of the times I couldn't help him, although I would have been happy to. To see the confused look on his face that day and the look he gave me, saying "help me" was more than enough to make me want to take his hand and get him out of there. I couldn't stand seeing the look of suffering on his face, even though it was, I suppose, important to the health system.

During the length of his affliction he was also to make many trips to the hospital for x-rays and other procedures that would crop up along the way. In 2008, before this all started happening, he had the misfortune to slip and fall on some ice while putting out the garbage can for pickup day. During this fall he broke some ribs, which the emergency doctor said should be healed up and good as new in six weeks.

After the allotted amount of time he was still not feeling well, so Carl returned to the emergency room once again. The doctor he had on this occasion sensed something wasn't right when he could feel a pulsing while poking around to find the cause of his pain. After ordering an ultrasound for the next morning, he knew his idea was correct. Carl had a huge aortal aneurysm and had to go to Winnipeg immediately for surgery. It was off to the races, with Corina doing the driving.

He was not allowed to leave the hotel room until the surgery. The doctor didn't want him on the streets in a car after he had examined him in Winnipeg. It was a large aneurysm. The anesthesiologist told my daughter that it was about 9.6 cm x 7 cm and it was pushing his kidneys apart, causing him to have problems, which had been ongoing, with his kidney functions. Usually when they reach the size of 4 cm they are considered dangerous and operated on for fear of them bursting.

This major surgery took a toll on Carl's health. He suffered a very slow recovery, with no appetite and generally ill health. He was hospitalized for almost a month and when he was discharged, he weighed a mere ninety-three pounds and could barely stand he was so weak. I often wonder, thinking back on this experience, could this have been a cause or maybe had a hand in his Alzheimer's? He had an incision from stem to stern; yes, it was major surgery, and my experience with anesthetic is that it's not always the greatest thing for some people, although it is a very necessary tool for surgery.

In his frail condition, he was loaded back into the car again for the long journey home. This is one time when I wondered *how does a person qualify for a plane ride?* This would have been a much more comfortable and faster way of transporting him, I'm certain. I wonder what it was about my gentle husband that didn't qualify him for the medical perks that are out there. Let me know; settle my curiosity.

Another major scare for me happened on our 50th anniversary. It all started with Carl getting up from his "big chair" and going down the hallway to the "little boy's" room. Of course, I followed him down there. It was now two years since he had been diagnosed with the big one. I always went along with him in case he needed an extra set of hands to get him safely back to his chair again, making sure he met the dress code and didn't have an unnecessary fall.

When he made it to the washroom, he started drooling and began to collapse on me. I quickly half carried him back to the living room and laid him down on the chesterfield, then made my first 911 call. He was picked up by the ambulance and taken to the emergency room at our local hospital. His condition quickly deteriorated and the doctor on call at the time, plus the emergency nurses, were scrambling trying to sort out what was wrong with my little buddy.

They had a fairly new method which was a big help in dealing with this crisis. They were to bring in specialists from Thunder Bay via a TV screen. This was happening in the room where Carl was stationed, with them observing the proceedings and offering advice to help out the doctor. I was also able to answer any of their questions that were to arise. To me, it was a needed improvement in the health care system.

The outcome to all of this worry was that Carl had gone septic. The cause of this was an infection in his bladder, if I remember correctly. He had a very weak immune system, most likely caused by taking harsh medications for his rheumatoid arthritis over the years. Once he was being treated and in stable condition, he was admitted to a room in the hospital, hooked up to IVs and a heart monitor.

The doctor told me later that if he hadn't gotten to the hospital when he did, he wouldn't have lasted for more than two hours. This isn't how I imagined us spending our 50th Anniversary. Once he was admitted, he spent two weeks recovering and was still taking antibiotics when he was discharged. While a patient, the doctor was very kind to him, taking him for a walk one day. He also settled him down when he grew agitated as was prone to happen now at this stage of his Alzheimer's. This was mostly caused by being hooked up to the IVs and the monitors. The "clothes pin" on his finger monitoring his oxygen levels was pretty much a lost cause at this point as well.

While Carl was hospitalized, we were to receive another shock. His sister, Kay, whom he had an unusual close bond with, passed away three days after Carl was admitted. They were close in age, the youngest two of the Bolen family children. Kay was only two years older than Carl and the two of them had spent a great deal of time together in their growing up days.

Kay was the sister who was to enlighten me with information regarding Carl—like his small size, for instance. She had once told me how difficult it was when it came to purchasing clothing for him. When he was sixteen years old, he wore a size ten in children's clothes; this caused a few problems for finding something tasteful for a young man to wear which didn't portray a ten-year-old boy. Another bit that I was to hear from her was the story of his driving ability and his cap getting lost in the accident where they were to find themselves upside down on the gravel road.

Along with their closeness as children, they also shared some of the same problems when it came to their health. This is where the unusual part comes into the picture. Kay had succumbed to cancer which was discovered in her kidney earlier when she and Carl were both in the hospital together having similar procedures performed by the same specialist. Carl had his procedure done first and Kay had hers next. They were both in the recovery ward at the same time, just a few beds from each other.

Now to think he was to have a near death experience with a bladder infection, was hospitalized and would then lose his sister three days later was difficult to understand. They had similar health experiences when they were both discovered to have aneurysms; both were sent to Winnipeg, Manitoba for major operations. The surgeries were performed by the same surgeon: a popular specialist in this field and maybe the only person qualified to do this procedure practicing near the Rainy River and Thunder Bay districts. Kay was first to go and then Carl was to follow later on. This left me wondering about these two special siblings and what they went through together in the course of their lives.

It was going to be a difficult task to tell Carl about losing Kay, especially at this point when he was still weak and had a long road ahead to recovery. Fearing that it may cause him to go into a state of depression, I confided with his doctor, making sure that this devastating news wouldn't cause him a major setback. The doctor agreed with me and suggested that I tell him now while he was getting medical treatment. With Alzheimer's, it was difficult to know what his reaction might be.

He was to miss Kay and was sad after hearing this news. Later on, after his recovery, we took him to Thunder Bay to her grave site to enable him to pay his respects. When he reached the stage of being bedridden, he told me that on more than one occasion he could actually see her and talk to her. His special angel was coming to visit her special brother.

CHAPTER THIRTEEN

Our Fight for Sanity

Again, Carl was to have another setback. It seemed like he couldn't escape these health scares. This one took place on December 14, 2015 and involved an emergency trip back to the hospital in Thunder Bay after being there for a procedure earlier that afternoon.

Following the afternoon procedure, we had made our way to Carla's home. A short while later, we were on our way to a hockey game. Keighan was playing and we were excited to watch the game. This was always an enjoyable experience for us since our two grandsons played hockey and we were able to finally watch real, live games, cheering on our boys.

After getting Carl bundled up with cozy blankets, we were set for some good old-fashioned hockey. Things were to change quickly with Carl beginning to shiver, almost violently it seemed. We quickly had to change our plans and take him out of the arena and head for home. Once again, his condition was to deteriorate rapidly with his stomach in an upset mood. It was off to the emergency room once more with a very sick Grandpa.

Graesen came along with us, assisting his Grandpa, getting him into a wheelchair and helping with the signing in at the nurse's station. Carl was quickly assigned a doctor. After much testing and working on him for six hours, he was once again to be admitted, fighting for his life.

We were under the impression that he had another bladder infection, but we weren't told until he was discharged that he had gone septic once again. The doctor told my daughter that he must have nicked him accidently during the afternoon procedure, causing bacteria to enter his system. We weren't told this until he was being discharged two weeks later on Christmas Eve with a charge of antibiotics.

The road to recovery was to be a rough one, taking its toll on his body. This was not a good thing, especially since he had Alzheimer's on top of everything else. His health problems brought to mind the time he was hit in the stomach with the sledgehammer. This—along with the broken ribs, the aneurysm and now two bouts of septic shock—was a lot for one body to take.

The results of these heavy-duty health challenges were nothing short of a miracle—he actually survived and went on to recover. They were a test of his mettle for sure and brought to mind the note his mother wrote many years earlier asking him if he was still as tough as ever. The way his life was unfolding, he had to be tough if he was to survive.

We stayed at Carla's home for a period of recovery. There, Carl had a special job to keep him busy and to keep his brain occupied: folding clothes and folding socks—lots of them that needed to be matched up! Some were missing, so it proved to be challenging for him. He was happy sitting all day doing this chore. He couldn't believe all the different socks that the grandchildren had, more than enough, he thought. The following day he would start back at it again, never seeming to tire or become bored with this important task.

I think nursing homes should use this method of keeping residents occupied. It would be something they enjoy as well as keeping them busy, giving them a sense of purpose, and leaving them feeling needed. Working with the different colours, textures, and patterns would be sure to put them in a happy place.

He also enjoyed working on the larger piece puzzles (larger pieces made them easier to pick up). Sitting with him and giving him a hand kept him interested, and there were times when he would make a piece fit if it didn't. He was certainly ingenious in solving problems that arose during the course of his illness: like, for example, making a hole in the front of his pullups so he didn't have to pull them down when the need to "pee-pee" was to strike. He could be very innovative when it came to doing something that he had been doing all his life and now proved a challenge for him with the onslaught of Alzheimer's.

The simple task of tying shoelaces could still be done, taking lots of time, and maybe with the bow at the beginning of the shoe instead of at the top near the ankle where it normally would be. He lost interest in his favourite television shows, though, not being able to concentrate on what was happening.

At one point he was an avid reader, enjoying western novels, having read all the books put out by Louis L'Amour. I had given all his books away earlier to an elderly lady friend who I had met while working at Cherie's Café. She had mentioned to me on an occasion that she enjoyed reading western novels. Carl was happy to pass them on to Mrs. Olga Tolten who was overjoyed to receive them.

This chapter of my time spent with Carl and dealing with this Alzheimer's invasion was difficult at times (our life as we knew it was changing). There were times that caused me pain just to see what was happening now that the disease was progressing. It hurt my heart to see him suffering. At other times, something would happen that was laughable, to say the least. And then there were "things" going on that were unbelievable during the course of a day.

Some of the incidents caused tears from watching him and seeing the deterioration progressing, knowing that, short of a miracle, he wasn't going to survive. Then again, there was a closeness that Carl hadn't lost, like when he would hold my hand and want to talk all night long. Thinking back, there was also that time when he hugged me too tight I thought my ribs were going to break!

Some of it would cause a scare for me. The scary incidents, besides the crashes, usually happened during the night when he had a habit of causing me to take fright, scaring the daylights out of me!

There were times when I had to take the apron off, meaning I had to fight for him, speak out for him, and stand in front of him ready to do battle to protect his dignity...especially when he couldn't stand up for himself. There were incidents that caused me to dial 911 in a panic on more than one occasion to get him to the emergency room to have the medical team look him over.

It frustrated me when my word wasn't taken literally, especially when it came to his care. I learned to scrutinize and closely monitor his medications and note any changes to his personality. With his liver now failing, he was unable to properly digest certain drugs which would build up in his system causing an upset to his normal behaviour. Sometimes this caused him to sleep for three days non-stop; or on the flip side, he would stay awake for days on end.

Often, he could be left in an agitated state not being in his usual happy frame of mind. There were times when I was left in a happy place, knowing Carl was being cared for at home in a familiar setting with faces he recognized. This, for me, was a good enough reason to be happy!

There was lots of learning involved. Taking the time to delve into the challenges Carl was having and seeing if I could correct or make them better was essential. For example, in dealing with a variety of strong infections—like E. coli which caused him to go septic—he needed to be put on Septra for three weeks, not two, or it would come back to haunt him.

I mentioned to our nurse Carla that he wasn't sleeping well, and I wondered if taking melatonin would help the problem. You bet his little brown boots it helped! This is what Carla found out for me. Alzheimer's patients lack melatonin which messes up their sleep patterns which causes increased agitation and restlessness. Several studies were conducted showing that seven out of ten patients showed remarkable improvement taking melatonin.

So, we got Carl started on a program to bring up his level of melatonin, and his sleep pattern improved. I found out that melatonin has been used on Alzheimer's patients since 1995 and has resulted in significant improvements in their sleeping habits and decreased amounts of "sundowning" (late-day confusion). There was less agitation.

On the third night after getting his system built up, he slept all night long. What a happy occasion that was! This was something I learned and tried with the doctor's okay, which saved both Carl's and my sanity. I only started this program after he had become bedridden. If only I had known earlier, it may have taken the run out of his walk and kept him safer.

CHAPTER FOURTEEN

Inside the Injured Mind

In this chapter I do something you may find different: I slip into Carl's mind. I imagine going around with him on his daily adventures along with the possibility of mishaps and try to figure out what he was thinking. In case you have forgotten, Carl called me "The Boss" in our later years when I was in charge of his well-being and acted as his power of attorney (you could say I called the shots). At this time, I begin this little adventure from Carl's perspective.

Sometimes lately I find my Grandpa crossing my mind lots. I think he will definitely be having something to say when I get to heaven, that's for sure. Some more of this Charlie stuff, like "Charlie, what the devil were you thinking? Don't you know better than to do that?"

Me and Grandpa—we had a good thing going on back then. He sure didn't try to slow me down any. He let me be a boy on my own terms. There is a song that keeps running through my mind. Note that I said "mind." It's called "Life is a Dance." One of the lines in this song is "Life is a dance; you learn as you go." We have certainly been learning lots, the Boss and I. Not all of it good, but educational nevertheless. I'm sure we could "Waltz Across Texas" with Ernie Tubb quite easily with the knowledge that we picked up along the way.

We used to enjoy a little bit of dancing, especially those polkas. Boy we could polka until we could barely breathe back in the day. We got so good at it that we didn't even step on each other's toes. Now you can't beat that, can you! It got to the point where I would ask the Boss to dance before she hinted to me that we shouldn't be wasting that good music. Yes, it was a nice change from working all the time. It gave us a bit of a chance to get a little close to each other.

One annoyance of mine was when one of the professionals who worked with me casually made the comment to avoid falls. If I was to break a hip it could be the end of me or put me on my back for a long period of time with my toes pointing to the sky once more. The difference would be that I would be lying on the bed looking at the ceiling. I wouldn't have my brown boots on this time.

No, I don't think this would be a good outcome. You just never can tell what can happen if you were to crash land. I don't think the "Boss" would like to find out either. I was to become skilled at it, though. In fact, I maybe planned my trips, truth be told. Like the night at Carla's house. She is my oldest daughter and the nurse in the family, which comes in handy, for me anyway. She's fast on her feet, too. The night I'm going to tell you about in particular happened at her house: my first fall.

She has a nice new house; a split level I think you could call it. She almost beat me down the stairs, after being jolted awake from a dead sleep in the middle of the night from a loud crash. That scared the daylights out of everyone! That's a darn good feat for anybody. Anyway, me and the Boss always stayed in Graesen's room. He was very kind and let us sleep in his bedroom whenever we came to the city for a visit. He had all of his hockey memorabilia from over the years displayed around the room and together we always enjoyed checking it out.

Now, his bedroom was about seven steps down from the kitchen—right off the family room—with a bathroom next door. This was handy for me. There was also another area about seven steps down, across from the bedroom. It was the basement. Are you getting the picture? I don't know if I was being adventurous again or what, but in the dark, I got confused, getting the bathroom door and the basement door mixed up. Maybe I just forgot, lost my train of thought.

Boy! What a racket that created! I think I actually went over the side of the stairs, part way down after throwing myself off balance when reaching around the corner for a light switch. This was my usual routine when getting up during the night to answer the call of nature. It was a routine I was familiar with, but then I was usually standing on the floor area and not at the top of a set of stairs.

After the girls surveyed the scene later, they came to the conclusion that the loud explosion was caused from the contents of a shelf I had uprooted on my trip downhill which landed on the cement floor. And from me, of course! I could hear the feet hit the floor that night before the light came on and lit up the room.

Carla came down two flights of stairs so fast to get to the crash site. She knew it was me. Her nursing instincts came into play; she almost pushed the Boss out of the way so she could survey the scene of the crash. Four eyeballs round as saucers were peering at me there on the floor.

Where I ended up landing was to be another interesting factor. My landing pad was in front of the cat's litter box, on my hands and knees with a sheepish grin on my face once again. There was a bit of a scrape on my chin, and my knee needed a bit of attention. Other than that when my personal nurse finished with her examination, I was good to go. Once more that bony little hip had been spared—I escaped in one piece.

Thinking about it later, I wonder whatever happened to the "call of nature" mission that I was on? I was to certainly land in a perfect spot, don't you think? What with the cat litter box directly in front of me? If I had been in an adventurous mood, I might have planned it that way. All I can say at this time is I wonder how this scene would have played out if there was a cat using the litter at the time of my crash? Most likely different...if a cat gets a good scare, their claws usually come out. There could have been a bit more blood loss!

Following this first fall of mine, a while later I was at the hospital for some further testing once again. They asked me a few questions before they proceeded with the MRI or the cat scan—whichever one it was at the time. I had both of them on more than one occasion, so I tend to get confused at what they might have planned for me. All I know is that between me and the Boss—mostly me—we made journeys to Thunder Bay seventeen times in one year. Can you beat that? It's no surprise that I forgot what I was there for!

Getting back to the questions, one of them was, "Have you had any falls lately?" I told them, "Yes, I had. I fell down a well once." They showed concern on their faces and left for the waiting room to question the Boss for details, hoping to get the story from her.

The next time I was to have more testing done, they asked me the same question again. "Have you had any falls lately?" Forgetting about falling down the well, I told them, "Yes. I'd fallen down a chimney." Once again, they rushed out with concern on their faces with questions regarding my answer, making sure they were getting the facts straight. It was dark and similar to a tunnel, that's all I could remember. Tomorrow if someone were to ask, I might call it something else. That's how I operate. I guess that's one, and probably the only perk I get from having Alzheimer's disease: the ability to tell stories—some of them believable, some of them not.

The result of falling down the "cat litter dungeon" was that a chesterfield would be pushed up against the basement door at bedtime with hopes of preventing me from trying this again. This was to be the beginning of the crashes. Once they started, there seemed to be no end to them. How can a person abuse their body so much, then turn around and do it all over again? Maybe it's got something to do with this new sickness, this "Alzheimer's" thing. It's been causing me some pain and humiliation, that's for sure. I feel rather lucky, not having broken anything so far. That could very easily happen one of these days.

Do you remember that song, "Walk Out Backwards"? Boy, it sure doesn't work for me when I'm walking backwards! It usually means I'm heading for a fall, another one of my noisy landings, causing a bit of a stir...

The Boss will come on the run, a worried look on her face, most likely thinking: this is the end of his hip for sure. She will get me up on my feet again, give me a good check over, sometimes with me ending up in the shower. She tells me this is the way she can tell for certain if there are any bruises or bleeding that could be concerning. I think she may even check "Willy Wonka"; though she says she has to wash him also. I used to do that trick myself but now I let her. I may lose my balance or something and there's certainly no use going around on my daily adventures smelling like pee-pee, is there? Besides, one never knows where I may end up.

Speaking of walking backwards, why do I tend to pick up speed when falling down? I don't know the answer to this question. Maybe I'm flying low? It's a whole new kettle of fish, that's for sure. No boiled suckers either. I should try to slow down a bit, or maybe rig myself with some kind of a parachute, something to slow me down when I'm on the way to a crash landing. I would then have a better chance of not bruising or breaking anything.

But then thinking back on events, I can have a rough landing falling forward also, so I would be kept busy trying to man the controls of this parachute. I can just hear my grandpa again. He's probably thinking, "Charlie, where are you going now?"

That reminds me of something: another country song. Can you tell we still enjoy country music? This goes back to day one. I think it keeps our hearts happy. We have Sirius radio in our home and also in her vehicle set to come on to "Willie's Roadhouse" to the good old-fashioned country tunes that we both grew up enjoying. Sometimes I like to sit in front of the radio and just listen; they can take you back to yesterday once more. Truer words were never spoken. It's a good idea to have something in common when you ask the "big question."

Country music is here to stay for us as a couple. You can always have a dance if you want, or you can dance to your own tune. Whatever suits your fancy. Before I forget what I was going to say about that other song, it was about having it all figured out. It went like this: "I had it all figured out—WRONG!" That's another good one for me to think about. It reminds me of some of my moves that don't work out the way I planned.

It sure is nice to like country music. You can listen to the Grand Ole Opry on a Saturday night. You can pretend you're somebody in a song, shed a few tears for the pain they are going through. You can cuddle up, let your mind wander, and just enjoy it. It's all good stuff!

Besides liking country music, another thing I enjoy doing is talking. It doesn't hurt to talk; there is no pain involved. I enjoy telling stories. I talk to the Boss at night when I forget that it is bedtime. I like to hold her hand too when I'm talking. We have some good conversations, me and the Boss. One night I told her that I had walked to Emo that day. She questioned me about my trip, wondering what I wore on my feet being it is quite a hike from the farm to Emo. I told her that I had worn my brown boots.

When I was a boy, I enjoyed walking, especially if I had my brown boots on. They made me feel manly, I think. I like to mention my good friends when I'm talking, even though she gently reminds me that some of them have passed away, gone to heaven. That doesn't stop me, though. I'll mention them again tomorrow night. It doesn't hurt.

There are times when I like to work at night, too. I seem to forget that I can barely walk, but that doesn't stop me from thinking that I can work. I get up during the night and check out the front window to see if someone is waiting to pick me up. She will tell me that it is Saturday, and no one is working. I am happy to hear that and go back to bed with her.

Maybe I didn't want to work in the first place. I'm thinking that a person gets used to working and just doesn't want to stop. Later I may get up again and check to see if the work truck is still parked out front at the roadside. The Boss will tell me that someone came and picked it up earlier. I happily go back to bed again.

The Boss knows how to settle me down and stop me from worrying. I think she needs a nap; she has been looking tired lately. I don't know why. I'm not tired, so why would she be? When she "crashes" it usually means that she is having a quick power nap, something to revive her, give her some energy. Maybe I keep her too busy, I'm not sure.

When I "crash" it means something else: nothing to do with sleeping. No, I'm just having one of my falls; maybe I was trying out that walking backward trick again. Lord, life can be strange sometimes! It's not how you want to do something. It's just how it turns out. She finally fell asleep! I got excited! Now I could have some fun without getting caught!"

This is when I like to sneak around and see what kind of fun I can have, or in other words, mischief I can get into. That's what it usually is when I'm involved. On this particular occasion, I got out of my pajamas and got myself all dressed up. After putting on my shoes and jacket, I quietly left the house on a small adventure.

I don't know where I was headed, but I ended up at the neighbour's house. The nice man there, I remember his name was Art, helped me get back home to where I lived. He was a kind person and helped us out whenever he could, shovelling snow and other things around our yard. Another man who lives on the corner across from us is very kind to us as well, cutting our grass and other jobs where he can. He also tilled the garden for us and made her happy. His name is Harvey. It is nice when you have good neighbours, especially now when I can't help much.

Getting back to that incident when I escaped custody, you could call it... when we arrived at my door and rang the doorbell, I could hear her feet hit the floor. The door flew open and a very surprised Boss was standing there, not even aware that I was gone. Nope, I was out gallivanting, getting some fresh air, you might say. It was nice of my neighbour to get me safely back home again. Good neighbours make the world a better place to live. Everybody should be so lucky.

This was the end of my visiting even though I thought it was fun, sneaky to say the least, when some trick door knobs showed up! They fit over the regular ones and make it almost impossible for me to escape nowadays. She can get the door open, but even while watching her, when she doesn't realize that I am of course, I still can't figure them out. A mean trick is all I have to say about this invention. The Boss disagrees with my opinion and tells me they are "clever."

I enjoyed going exploring. I'm sure I could have been another Marco Polo, or better yet, may have hopped on board ship with Columbus as most of my exploring had to do with water or rather "waterworks" you might think. Toilet water, that is.

This incident that I am going to share with you was to happen once again at Carla's home, in the darkness, during the night. Once again, I was trying to find the bathroom and got headed in the wrong direction. At this point I was getting good at heading in the wrong direction. This was a downfall for me and caused me a bit of pain and embarrassment.

It also caused a lowering effect on my ego at the time, leaving me in deep thought after some of my exploring mishaps. They ended up finding me standing in front of the large screen TV in the family room. When they apprehended me, I said, "What a piss off!"

Now that I'm thinking about it—my comment that is—maybe it could have been called that if they hadn't caught me when they did. That's probably what they were thinking, also. It may have ended up with the mops and buckets coming out for some cleaning practice. Of course, by this time I would have been safely lying in bed, tucked in nice and cozy doing more of my heavy thinking. Thinking and waiting patiently for the Boss to return. Then I could finally do some more of my talking that I was awfully fond of. I would hold her hand again and just get at it. Maybe talk some more about my friends, some from long ago. I wonder now…was this a way to change the subject after what had just happened? "Clever," she is probably thinking!

I was to go on another exploring expedition…this time at my home in Atikokan. This incident was another Columbus expedition for me, involving water once again, or more truthfully "waterworks." This time I ended up in the mudroom, the room where the kitchen garbage container is kept. Made from wood, it stood about three feet high and was painted. I think she bought it at a craft shop, and if I remember correctly, the Boss was quite fond of it. This would have been a perfect receptacle for what I had in mind, if I would have opened the lid.

This caused a bit of a stir and left me thinking, what next? Yes, there was a next time; this is while I was having my dinner and sitting in my favourite big chair. I like to call it "big" being it was almost too big for a small man like me. I always felt comfortable there. The Boss would roll up bath towels or blankets and stuff them around me to help me stay in place.

Dinner that evening was spaghetti and meatballs with lots of parmesan cheese, a favourite of mine. I don't know what happened this time, why I would do this, as foolish as it seemed after thinking about it later. I kicked in with the *"waterworks" once again right on top of my spaghetti! It was lucky the plate was on a pull up tray used for snacks and things like that. It didn't do much damage except spoil my supper. Lord, it's hard to be humble! The shame of it all!*

Years before this, I wasn't fond of spaghetti, even though my girls enjoyed it. They would play games with it while eating. They had fun sucking on the long strings as they would zip them into their mouth. I always said it reminded me of a plate full of worms. Maybe that brought back memories, I think...

This ended my exploring with Columbus, thank goodness! Getting back to the Boss being kind and trying to keep me out of trouble, she set up a series of five nightlights for me. If I left them alone and didn't touch them, they worked fine and did the trick. They started in the bedroom, next the hallway, bathroom, and finally into the kitchen. No more having adventures in the dark now if I stayed on the lighted path.

One night I went flying past the bathroom—you may already know I like to walk fast and sometimes I'm almost running. This time I only had one slipper on, and it was on backwards with my toes in the heel part. My other foot was bare. The one slipper made a loud slapping noise on the floor, sounding just like a beaver's tail hitting the water. The Boss was in the bathroom, sick. I forgot about her stomach problem—acid reflux, I think it was called. It usually bothers her in the night when she is trying to sleep. Just like me. Sometimes her medication doesn't make her feel better.

I shouted "OUT" to her on the way past with my one slipper flapping like crazy. I told her I was sure glad I didn't have any of what she had. I felt sad for a few minutes after saying that—after all, she was sick. I soon forgot about it as I was on a mission, heading to the kitchen for a cold drink. And a few good burps.

She taught me to burp after a drink, something about knowing that I had swallowed it and wouldn't end up choking when I laid down. After doing this for a while, I could burp really loud, almost scaring myself. This all happened on my way to the fridge, when I could still walk without falling down. Nowadays I don't get to the kitchen much. And I drink from a straw, the kind that bends. But I can still burp!

There's not much fun left for me, is there? I used to put my cream soda and orange pop in the oven after I had a few good swigs, along with a few good burps, of course. This part was always fun...this new trick. With storing my bottles in the oven, it was always wise to check it before turning it on. The possibilities of what could happen there are endless, besides the mess. This makes me think of where I hid the wine when I was a young lad. I enjoyed doing things different, unheard of, maybe. I could be the only one out there who likes to plan their moves, making life interesting.

Now, one night I came back to bed after one of those "fly by night" excursions, complaining. Not a happy camper, I woke up the Boss. She headed out to the kitchen not knowing what to expect. She checked out the refrigerator to see if I had a valid reason to be cranky. What she discovered was that I had grabbed the wrong bottle and had a few good swigs of soya sauce. It doesn't taste too bad if you put in on rice, but it's not nice if you drink it straight from the bottle.

It was after that eye-opener that she started to put things of that nature in safe places where they wouldn't be noticed so readily. This was just in case I was being adventurous again. For safety sake, much of my time is spent thinking these days. If you've ever gotten into mischief, maybe you'll know what I'm talking about. One night in particular while the Boss was busy doing her power nap thing, I got into a mess of trouble. This was to be the usual time for me, when the coast was clear.

I'm only telling you this because of this Alzheimer's thing, in case it might have happened to you too. Notice that I said "mess" of trouble. I went to the bathroom and removed my pull-up and take the credit for doing other things. Mistakes, you could say. Out of the ordinary things, if you're like me and get mixed up with your thinking. Sometimes I have a smidgen of an idea and that's where it stops.

That's what must have happened this time. She woke up, and sensing that I wasn't in bed, she panicked and came looking for me. Her eyes were big as saucers when she found me in the middle of this private inferno—at least that's what it seemed like at the time. The more I tried to clean up, the worse it got. After getting me all freshened up once more with a shower, I felt like new.

I like showers, especially when she puts my Old Spice deodorant on and rubs lotion on my legs and back. That always makes me smell better, like a million bucks better! If you smell good you feel good, that's what I find these days about myself. After the Boss got me all shined up and smelling good, she tucked me back in bed once again.

Yes…me and the Boss have a good thing going! She's my woman, and I'm her man. We are here for each other, helping each other out as much as we can. Back in bed there was no talking or whistling for me. This whistling was something new that I started doing when I was in a "bit of a jam." I think I was using it for a cover up. Maybe trying to pretend that I had nothing to do with the unfortunate happenings? I think the Boss was starting to catch on. There wasn't much I could hide from her these days. Only the two of us now, me and her, so who do you think is going to get the blame?

On this particular night, as I lay in bed, my thoughts went back to my grandpa. He wasn't around now to bail me out. I was sort of wishing that he was. Most likely he would have handled it a little bit different, but then he probably wouldn't have been able to give me a shower. I could imagine him scolding me again in his gentle manner like he would when I was a young boy: "Charlie, what happened? What were you thinking, Charlie?"

It took a good deal of time to shine things up in the bathroom. Lucky for her it was the bathroom, I was thinking. At least I got that part right. It sure is a good thing that I can think these days. I'm no darn good at walking, and it certainly doesn't hurt to think now, does it? Speaking of thinking, I'm beginning to think that I got lucky when I married the Boss. Who else would take such good care of me and keep me in that happy place?

She is a good cook, treating me to all my favourites, but there just doesn't seem to be a solution when it comes to fattening me up. It seems to be a lost cause for sure. At this point in time I weigh less than one hundred pounds, soaking wet with my long johns on. These are an important piece of my wardrobe, by the way. I'm always cold, even during the summer months.

Keep in mind that part of this weight is also due to the fact that I am carrying around a few litres of fluid in my abdominal cavity. This is apparently caused from my liver beginning to give up the ghost. Lord God, like I needed this new one to worry about! Me walking around with my belly sticking out from all the fluid gathering.

One of the many doctors told the Boss, when she was concerned for my well-being and worried that I was going to burst, that no, I wouldn't burst—it was just like being pregnant. No, it wasn't the same! You see, not being a female, I didn't have the proper container that you need for carrying a baby. I would also hope never to be pregnant if that's how it works. I suffered lots of pain from fluid collecting in my abdomen along with the breathing difficulty when laying down.

When all is said and done, I may as well fasten my seatbelt and go on this ride. It would probably be as nerve-racking as some of the rides I was to go on at the Lakehead Exhibition with Garfield when we were young and enjoying life.

Several medical professionals asked me if I was a drinker. This question seems to imply that you have to be a drinker in order to have this problem. It's as if, when I'm doing my thinking again, that maybe I should have been a drinker, seeing as I'm to end up like one anyway. But then again, maybe this wouldn't be such a good idea either. I wouldn't have been able to remember if I had had any fun or not. It's like I said earlier: life's a dance. You learn as you go.

Getting back to drinking, I will admit to having a root beer experience along with a certain liking for my cream soda and orange pop vigils in the middle of the night. Oh, and I can't forget the soya sauce episode—that was a real eye opener, one that wasn't to be repeated. I don't tend to mix my important drinks except that I'm partial to a good cup of coffee with lots of sugar and extra cream.

Now that I'm busy thinking, I'm wondering if the culprit could have been something that I ate. Maybe all the Planter's peanuts or the Oh Henry! chocolate bars? Who knows? I enjoyed eating them along with a Crispy Crunch now and then. Who is to know? Maybe I'm on to something here. Maybe I will have to do some investigating of my own.

It's off to face the next hurdle. Sort of reminds me of putting a show horse through its paces—the jumps seem to get more challenging as you go forward. Not easy for an old work horse like me who has already run too many races on the track! Oh well, bring them on, I say! The Boss will be here to help me out if I need her. She knows how to call 911 now, after having a few practice runs with me lying on the floor in a heap.

She will tell you about them later. There was lots of excitement and panic when these incidents happened. The ambulance boys and the one girl who were so attached to me knew how to flick on the siren after getting me loaded up. I rode in the back all cozied up with lots of blankets. They made my trips to the hospital as comfortable as possible. There wasn't much they could do about our famous potholes, though, so the speed limit was never broken on our journeys. It could have been fun if it wasn't for this problem. I had heard that the potholes were likely a result of the town being built on an area of muskeg. It was pretty much a losing battle trying to repair them. Yes, I think that they almost made us famous along with the iron ore find.

The loading up took place after putting me on a backboard with a cervical collar on to ease the pain, just in case the pain meant something was broken. They sure know their stuff and how to treat an old man whose legs don't want to go in the right direction anymore.

That describes me. They treat me so kind and gentle. This isn't just "a job" to them, you can tell. They put their heart into what they are doing and show concern and compassion for the unfortunate person who is on a journey to the emergency room. I was a lot like them with my gentle, caring ways. That is most likely why I found my wife, along with my blue eyes and captivating smile, of course.

The attendants were helpful. If I needed a bathroom break, they would assist me without hesitating. A couple of times they were to come to the house for a quick visit to check and see how I was doing, when I was back home, snuggled in my bed. I was richly blessed with getting to know them for sure. They always left me in a happy place. Being told that I had Alzheimer's had left me in a state of despair, not knowing what all was going to happen to me. The future looked bleak, but at this point in time, it wasn't to be all bad.

Being at home, I had my loved ones close, caring for me, keeping me company and not passing judgment when I would forget and make mistakes. Along with the paramedics who brought sunshine into my life, and the new people I met during the course of this new journey, all was turning out okay. Yes, all was good in the forest.

Graesen and Jaycelin visiting Grandpa in the hospital.

CHAPTER FIFTEEN

Start the Car!

Delving into Carl's mind has been an eye-opener. Getting into mischief and being his usual self when finding trouble was fun for him…I think! Trying to decipher what he may have been thinking has given me a whole new outlook on what went on in his mind.

This left me wondering at times—like on the morning I was sleeping at the foot of the bed so I could maybe hear him go past if he woke before me and was up to his sneaky stuff again. This time he stopped and tucked me in, something he would normally do when waking up first. Only this time he didn't stop tucking; he kept on going, making sure he had me totally under cover, going all around me, covering my head as well. I could barely breathe and thought the possibility of suffocating at this point was high.

I waited for him to leave the bedroom, most likely proud of the job he had just done. He was likely thinking to himself that no way was I going to get a chill! I waited as long as I possibly could before getting up and joining him.

He was standing in the middle of the kitchen floor and headed over to me, whispering. He said, "There's a dead body down the hall in one of the rooms. Someone is coming to pick it up."

That was a shock! That explained why he was particular in the way he covered me up. I was the dead body! Boy, I must have been sleeping sound for a while.

Another incident that left me wondering happened when we took him on a blueberry picking trip. My family from Thunder Bay were visiting. It was perfect timing for a quick trip to the patch so I could get this need to pick out of my system. Besides, Carl enjoyed eating blueberries and they are good for your health.

The grandchildren were sitting in the vehicle with Carl, keeping him company, listening to music, and eating snacks. I stayed close to the vehicle. I never knew how things may turn out when Grandpa took a notion to liven things up a bit.

A while later, Jaycelin came running to where I was picking, saying, "Grandma! Grandpa is out walking around. He said someone shot him in the leg."

That was the end of my picking for the day, my cue that it was time to head home. It was short and sweet. I did manage to get a few berries and Carl's leg was fine. Maybe he got a cramp in it from sitting. Who is to know? His imagination at this point could run wild.

Along with his imagination, he enjoyed running wild as well, especially during the night under the cover of darkness. This new trick of his could jolt me from being in a dead sleep to jumping up in shock and hollering. I guess you could call it that. This, in turn, would scare Carl and he would take off on the run down the hall to the bedroom where he must have felt safe, his little bare butt lighting up a path behind him.

What was taking place here, this new thing, was me falling asleep on the chesterfield, a much-needed power nap after getting him into bed and sleeping. I would have my head in the direction of the hallway, thinking my chances of hearing him, if he were to get up, were good. I wanted to prevent him from his need to explore during the night, which didn't always turn out for the best.

I don't know why, but he started this new thing of disrobing during the night—only from the waist down. I'm not quite sure why, nor does it really matter. Maybe just a new game of his... This startled me. For a man who was always cold, it was difficult to sort out. Maybe he just took a sudden notion to not wearing pull-ups, like he had had enough of that kind of nonsense. This would require him to take off his pajamas and his long johns.

The scares happened while I was sleeping and could sense someone standing in front of me. I would suddenly wake up, jump up, and holler from a good fright. This would likely scare anyone to life especially after seeing a bare little "willy" dangling a couple of feet from your face. My hollering would in turn scare him and set him off running to safety down the hall.

It didn't end there. Of course not! My job was to try to find his clothes...along with him helping me (it was cute). They could be anywhere. I checked the oven, but no, they weren't there. I guess that was reserved for his pop. I have to tell you the cleverest place I found the clothes was all folded up nice and neat stacked in the toilet bowl. His slippers were sitting perched on top, like the cherry on the cake, you could say. Who would think this quiet, gentle man could get such wild ideas?

I feel sorry for baring his soul, almost overcome with guilt while I'm writing, but I hope you are getting an idea of what my special man and I went through with this Alzheimer's thing. A sad state of affairs, for sure! That is how this disease works. It takes your dignity with it on the way down a rabbit hole in the dark.

It can play you out, but it doesn't stop at one thing. That love you had going all the way back to yesteryear and more, it makes it stronger with the need to keep your loved one safe, free from harm. This was to prove to be almost a lost cause at times.

With his belly swelling up and causing him pain, as well as interfering with his breathing, he was booked in at Thunder Bay for a drain procedure. The procedure was to take place with a specialist in a place where he had more of a chance if things were to go wrong.

Twice he fasted for this journey by air. For the first trip, we left in the morning. Carl was strapped down: not a comfortable way to go, but a safer one. We landed safely at the airport where we were to wait for an ambulance to transfer him to the hospital. After numerous calls and promises, no one came to pick him up. It got to the point where we were too late; the appointment wasn't going to be happening that day. After turning the plane around, we headed back to Atikokan where we were picked up by the boys once more and taken back to the hospital room.

At this point in time he had been a patient at the hospital for a lengthy period of time, close to a month, before he was discharged. By the time he arrived back to his room, he hadn't had anything to eat or drink because he had been fasting. It was now two o'clock in the afternoon. Also, Carl had been lying on a stretcher since morning, flat on his back in an old airplane.

I say old for a reason. The plane was old and rather scary: armrests were missing or partly missing, and the walls were scruffy. It looked like a hockey game had taken place inside. There were so many black marks on the walls. It got us there and back, but I was a little bit afraid and skeptical… The airplane was not the shiny orange one that lands at the hospital. It was a large white plane. I remember the "Bravo" part and was thinking, taking a look at my surroundings, that you would need a certain sense of "bravery" just to be a passenger.

As a first flying experience for medical reasons, this plane just didn't fit the bill as something the medical system should have been using for transferring patients. Maybe the government should look into things of this nature. Instead of taking from the medical care, start putting some money back into it. Seniors paid their dues over the years and it's time they were treated in a more humane fashion. That's my story and I'm sticking to it.

We tried this trip again a couple of days later, with the plane overshooting the Atikokan airport and not landing. I don't know what the cause was, if it was foggy or not, but they turned around and went back to Thunder Bay without us. Once again after fasting, Carl was returned to his room at the hospital. Some people have all the luck; some people have none.

After a few days, Carl was discharged from the hospital. Another appointment was made for him, only this time I was responsible for driving him there. This was to make certain he was going to get there, seeing the plane rides were not working out to his benefit.

The morning of the appointment arrived. We were almost set to leave the house, it was just a matter of pulling on a pair of jogging pants so Carl would be dressed for this adventure to the city. All was going fine until I tried to get his feet in the correct leg holes of the pants. I got him to stand and hold on so that I could pull them up. That's when everything was to go south. Carl let go and down he went with a crash! A nasty crash! He ended up lying in a heap on the floor in serious pain.

I dialed 911—the ambulance was on the way. I called Corina and Jaycelin and let them know what had happened. They hadn't left for school as it was not quite eight o'clock in the morning. The scene on the floor didn't look good, like there was a possibility he wasn't going to survive. Our friends the ambulance boys arrived and were so kind once again. With lots of care and Carl in much pain, they managed to get the cervical collar on and once again loaded him on the backboard for the trip to the hospital.

After a couple of hours in the emergency room with the doctor cutting his favourite blue plaid shirt sleeve open from the cuff almost to the collar to check for breaks, it was amazing that, for the amount of pain he had been in, nothing was broken. An abrasion on the back of his shoulder was all that was found. The pain by this time had settled down so the doctor gave us the go ahead to continue on to Thunder Bay to get this drain done. Maybe then his balance would be better and he wouldn't fall so easily.

So, off we went to Thunder Bay, Carl with his long johns on and his cut-up shirt sleeve blowing in the wind. No shoes on, either, just a blanket wrapped around him and his seat belt on. I have confidence while driving on the highway, so I stepped on the gas a bit, you could say. There was no way he was going to miss this appointment for the third time, come hell or high water! If that was the case, the possibility of him bursting would happen, I thought to myself.

Corina and Jaycelin followed me all the way; we had our own speedway going. Grandpa was sitting in the back seat not showing any concern whatsoever. To shorten this long story, we made it! Carla was waiting for us and off we went for the appointment.

We were waiting for him to come out to recovery and could hear him talking about being hungry. The nurse monitoring him gave him a bagged lunch, which he was quick to dive into. He was eating his dessert, an arrowroot cookie, when he said, "Start the car!" He was all set for another adventure, which drew smiles from all of us waiting for him. The fast ride I gave him mustn't have scared him! He was ready for more! No fear!!

CHAPTER SIXTEEN

The Last Candle

Someone once asked me, "What is so special about your husband that you're writing a book about him?" There is "lots" special about him. This man, my husband, was in an ambulance in the morning, in dire pain. Now it's all forgotten and he's back to his normal self, enjoying life along with a fast ride down the highway.

It's a good thing Mickey (his childhood dog) wasn't around today. He could have gotten more than he bargained for, trying to chase me speeding to Thunder Bay. It might have taken him an extra day to recuperate before he was able to get up and go again. Just like Carl and his big crash. This one is all in the past; now what can happen?

I had a new bathroom installed to make it safer for Carl. The new tub was a low stepper making it easier to get in and out, with surround bars on the tub. The tub had a heavy glass enclosure. This was to give him stability at the beginning, before he started losing his balance. At that point, it became a different story. I was to install a handheld shower which made it easier to wash his hair and rinse him off well. He was also now the owner of a new bath chair so that he could sit down and rest his legs while enjoying his shower. He loved this part of the day and would often want another shower later.

After getting him safely out of the tub, dried off, and smelling like Old Spice with his lotion rubbed on, it was "pull-up" time. For this, he would sit and there would be no problems, nor for the long johns, an important part of our daily procedure. It was always the bottoms that threw him off balance and he would fall.

Unfortunately, he was to have another fall, and once again I was dialing 911. I have a great fear of bleeding on the brain with the elderly, and it appeared to me that he had hit his head on a chair that I had stationed beside the toilet. The chair was for me to sit on when he was answering the call of nature. I could keep an eye on him in case he lost his balance and took a notion to fall off the toilet. We could talk to each other whenever given a chance. He loved to talk at this stage of the disease. Maybe we just had a lot of ground to cover making up for the "being quiet stuff" from the early years. And what are the chances of hitting your head on the chair that I sat on to prevent you from falling? Slim to none? Ironic, to say the least!

Everything turned out good once more regarding serious injuries. But while at the emergency room, he ended up having another drain from a doctor who gladly gave it a try and lightened some of the load for him. Once again, the boys brought him home and tucked him into his bed all cozied up and smiling.

Corina and I were also happy, after holding his hands and keeping him settled in the emergency department. At this point in time any intrusion of his space could possibly unnerve him. Corina and I were there to help the doctors make Carl feel safe, assure him that no one would harm him. Getting stressed out could bring out the "bear" in him at times. In this mode he could easily invent new cuss words. Not easy on the ears; nor not typical of this usually quiet man. These crashes of his were certainly harmful, to say the least.

October came, and with it, Thanksgiving. We all gathered at my house for a huge family feast, complete with the pumpkin pie and whipped cream that Carl was so fond of. Carl was seated at the table with us and wanted to try everything, enjoying himself, eating more than usual. He was happy, talking lots, putting smiles on the grandchildren's faces. This was his last meal at the table with his whole family surrounding him. He was happy at this time of celebration, giving us hope of more.

Next came November and his birthday. Once again, I was able to get him out of his bed to the kitchen table, sitting in his favourite chair with his birthday cake in front of him. Candles were lit up and glowing, with flames dancing as he watched them.

His attempt at blowing out his candles was to be a big event for him, but like all the times before, Jaycelin would sit on his lap and help him until the last candle was out. This was to be his last birthday...his last cake...his last candle.

———————

Now I'm crying again, but I'm telling you Carl's story from the beginning to where the story ends. Some of the events that were to happen to Carl while he was still able to walk were to prove interesting, as well as sad at the same time. While I was still working, before Carl's illness came to light, I had the idea that he was missing clothing, which proved to be true. I found a plastic bag full of rags downstairs in the furnace room. Inspecting them, I found a few pairs of his long johns with the outside leg seams cut off but with the legs still attached to the waistband. This was some of the missing clothing—his special attire that he wouldn't be without even in the summer months. These long johns were expensive. I think they were for skiing: two-ply and cozy.

Some of his hats were also on the missing list. I finally found them two years later. Two of them were what he called his "fur balls." When we couldn't find them, I went out and bought him a new one. He enjoyed wearing them in the winter months as they had a good fit as far as hats were to go; they usually never fit him. I also came across a cardboard box full of his pants in the storage room with the Christmas decorations. Some of them were new with the price tags still on. He must have kept himself busy during the day.

It was a good thing I got off work at two o'clock in the afternoon. Once while I was standing at the kitchen sink doing dishes, he had been standing a short distance behind me, talking. When I turned around, flames were shooting over his head from his back and he was unaware of this. He had a bad habit of turning the stove element on and backing up to it to get warm. This time his shirt had caught on fire! I grabbed him and turned the spray hose on him. He escaped with no burns, just a hole in one of my favourite shirts.

Standing near the stovetop was one of the ways he tried to warm up, being cold all the time. I'm thinking this was from his rheumatoid arthritis. He also used this method to heat up his hands and wrists when they were swollen and painful. I was to find two more shirts with holes in the back and also a pair of pajama bottoms with the telltale holes of fire. At this point, I didn't hesitate to "throw in the towel" at work, to devote my time to keeping my little man safe.

Once I was to find money tucked into a pair of his socks when I was in the process of putting them on him. After checking a few more pairs, I found some more. A total of one hundred and forty dollars that he had squirrelled away in his sock drawer! Tidy sum to say the least! That could buy more than a few good cups of coffee along with some of his favourite butter tarts.

Maybe this hoarding money had something to do with a comment he had made to Carla. We were leaving in my vehicle to go somewhere with Carla doing the driving and Carl sitting in the passenger seat beside her. I had run back to the house after discovering that I had forgotten something. Carl asked her why we were waiting, and Carla told him that they were waiting for me. In his clever mode, he said, "She's probably getting my wallet. She took it from me on the day we were married, and I haven't seen it since." He was good at throwing out small barbs. He reminded me of a bantam rooster—harmless but very effective!

Another incident that happened during this period when he was still on the go was him heading to Corina's house, almost on the run, to tell her Jaycelin hadn't gotten off the school bus. Poor Grandpa! He was in a panic, worried about his granddaughter. At this time, she was riding to school with her mom and not riding on the bus, but that didn't stop her Grandpa from worrying about her.

Just lucky for us that he didn't fall down and seriously hurt himself on this run. One thing about his journey with Alzheimer's was that his heart was always in the right place. His love and kindness would always shine through, even if his mind was off kilter. This shining through helped us immensely when dealing with this disease.

———⁓ɷↄↄↄↄↄↄↄↄↄ⁓———

There was another event that turned out to be interesting, to say the least—a short vacation with Corina and Jaycelin to Duluth. Grandpa and I tagged along with them for a "get away." Thinking back, it was our last adventure with Grandpa that we could call a vacation, of sorts. It was planned, and we hoped it would be a pleasant holiday.

The room was booked at the Edgewater, a popular fun-filled water park with lots of cool events for water lovers. Off we went! Road trip! Corina, Jaycelin, Grandpa with Alzheimer's, and me.

After getting safely through the border with Grandpa, we stopped not far down the highway at a perfect rest stop. There was a large shop there with lots of different snacks and souvenir items that catered to travellers. Jaycelin bought herself a package of sour cotton candy. After having a pinch, I couldn't see where the sour idea was coming from. The next time the package was to come over the back of the seat to the front, I tried some more. This time I reached down towards the bottom of the bag for another pinch, thinking that maybe the sour was on the bottom of the bag, settled. I was correct. It was ALL down on the bottom! After choking, coughing, and having difficulty breathing, I knew I was right again! I wasn't sure if I was going to survive; I wasn't good.

That wasn't all. Halfway to Duluth, we stopped for some lunch. It was supposed to be a pie place, so I got the idea it was going to be a pleasant experience…but I was wrong. I thought most everything on the menu wasn't from our planet. We weren't familiar with anything. Starving, I ordered radish soup, knowing what a radish was but not at all what the soup might be. To this day I don't know what anyone else ordered or if they were to order at all. My soup came and it looked like pureed radishes. I ate some. I was starving and might not survive until we reached Duluth.

Needless to say, but because I'm telling the truth here, the soup kicked in. We weren't quite to Duluth yet, to the safety of our room, when my belly started rebelling, having an adverse reaction to this radish soup. Lord God, I managed to stay safe until we made it into our hotel room. I shall leave the rest up to your imagination. Later on, it was Grandpa's turn to act up.

He had been good up until now, and he was about to make up for it. He wanted out of that room, and once he had an idea, he wasn't going to give up on it. He said it was just a big cult and he was leaving. That was a new one; I had a problem figuring that one out. He was getting noisy and disruptive, with us trying to settle him down. He slept for a short while and went back to trying to escape.

One of the concerning things was that he was trying to get the adjoining door open. I'm surprised we didn't get a knock on the door—it would have been well deserved if we would have. The only thing that kept him sitting on the bed after he was all packed up was the fact that he couldn't find his jacket. This was after I had told him that his jacket was really mine, which settled him down. He wasn't going anywhere without his jacket.

The next day went much better with everyone going to the mall to do some shopping for Jaycelin. It was a fun thing and necessary before school was to start up. I stayed with Grandpa Carl, letting him have some space but still keeping an eye on him. All was forgotten of his shenanigans from the night before. Another storm had blown past. Now it was my turn to act up again. After being called "old lady" by a little boy getting on the elevator in the Edgewater hotel, which dampened my spirits a bit, not thinking that he had any reason to call me old. My hair might be gray, but that's no cause to be passing judgment, that's for sure. I think he was just in need of someone to teach him some manners and right about then I would have been the perfect person for the job, but I smiled and kept on going.

That evening my knee was acting up and continued to get worse. If you've ever had frozen shoulder, you'll know what it's like—I'm sure I had frozen knee. I couldn't bend it; the pain was severe. Just breathing seemed to cause me pain. And the height of the bed didn't help. It must have been close to my armpits it was so high. I thought once more that I was going to die trying to climb up onto it. Then how do you get comfortable?

In case you've forgotten, the first time I thought I was a goner was after the sour cotton candy experience when I couldn't breathe. Then it was the radish soup. The next morning, we checked out of our room and headed home, after first visiting the zoo. I was so tired that I only wished for some pain-free sleep. Corina had to locate a wheelchair to take me out of the room and get me to the vehicle; that's the kind of shape I was in! Once we got to the zoo it was off to find another wheelchair to get me out of the car and on to the paved pathways to check out the sights. Corina went ahead of us to see what she could find of interest. Jaycelin, meanwhile, was trying her best to push me in the chair.

To add beauty and interest to this idyllic spot, there was a creek running alongside the walkway along with some beautiful pine trees. Grandpa was under the trees interested only in picking up pinecones and filling his pockets. Meanwhile, Jaycelin was having problems trying to maneuver the wheelchair along the winding paved path that went downhill because of the weight difference between her and me (with me tending to weigh quite a few pounds more). It was difficult to get it stopped on the downhill grade. For a while I was afraid that I was going to end up in the creek or maybe upside down on the path with the wheelchair racing on without me!

It all ended well with me parked on the trail with the brakes on and Grandpa sitting on a bench beside me resting. Corina and Jaycelin continued on alone to see what the zoo had to offer (besides me). I was also lucky that Grandpa Carl didn't try his luck at pushing me. The possibilities of both of us landing in the creek would have been high if one was taking bets on it. Everything seemed to be happening to me on this trip. It certainly wasn't proving to be a relaxing vacation like I had planned.

Corina got me safely loaded up into the back seat of our vehicle and off we went, headed for home. On the way, hunger overcame us once more. This time, Corina stopped at a Dairy Queen, a place that was familiar to all of us hungry travellers. Even Carl recognized it. He was the first one out of the vehicle, wasting no time to get inside. Corina and Jaycelin rushed to keep up to him.

I was left, forgotten you might say, in the back seat of the vehicle with my frozen knee. I made my way to the door trying to hop, with a few curious looks from others who were stopping. The place was packed, standing room only. Carl pushed his way up to the counter ignoring the line ups. He was on a mission, and he was making sure he was going to get noticed. When the server asked him what he would like, he said, "a cheeseburger with no burger." This caused a few smiles, but that's what he got—the makings of a good cheeseburger without the burger. This journey with Carl was to teach everyone a lesson. Don't be surprised: you never know what might happen or what he might say.

After this burgerless break, it was on the road again towards Thunder Bay. My knee still hadn't improved, and the pain was unbearable. We passed customs once more and made our way to Carla's home. She gave me one of the boy's broken hockey sticks to use to take the weight off my knee when having to walk. Perfect! I mentioned later that the two grandsons should start up a business making walking sticks out of broken hockey sticks. They most likely had a few of them after all the hockey they played!

The girls still talk about our holiday and poke fun at me. It was my turn, I guess, for all of the nasty things that happened. They especially liked the radish soup portion. Lord, that was nasty! There was a lesson to be learned here, wasn't there? Corina liked to call our little adventure a "Griswold vacation" (based on the National Lampoon's Vacation movies). That was to be our last family road trip with Carl. After the first night he settled down and seemed to enjoy it along with his pockets full of pinecones.

His last birthday, Nov 29, 2017, trying hard to blow out the candles.

Carla enjoying her father's company.

CHAPTER SEVENTEEN

The Apron Comes Off

The following summer I had a ramp built for Carl. It was much safer pushing him down the ramp in his chair than trying to get him down the steps and out to the vehicle if we wanted to go exploring—deer watching and such. Along with the ramp came a new deck as well. The ramp, in order to be safe, requires a gradual slope to it, not just a downhill incline.

Along with this I purchased a new transfer chair for him, one with rubber tires and brakes on the handles. His previous one had brakes on the back wheels, but try putting them on when going down a ramp! There was a good possibility of ending up on the neighbour's lawn before I would get the chair stopped. Not a ride Carl would enjoy.

The only time he enjoyed going fast was on the highway, with me driving him above the speed limit after he had given me the green flag and hollered, "Start the car!" Sort of like our own personal Grand Prix. Only instead of "Start your engines!" there was only one car to start. Why be old and boring? Why not old and foolish? It's bound to be more fun—ask me sometime. There's no reason to grow up too fast…is there? Like George Jones tells us in one of his songs, "I don't need no rocking chair." We should get old at our own speed and not before.

After Carl's last birthday celebration on November 29, 2017, his health seemed to deteriorate. It was apparent to me that his issues with Alzheimer's and now his liver not working properly were beginning to take a toll on him. A great deal of time was spent sitting in his big chair snuggled up with blankets or lying in his bed. Thoughts of Christmas were in the air when Carl was to have his last big crash. At this point he was still able to walk, but I was always with him, staying close by just in case. I had gotten up and left him sleeping, safely, I thought, for a few minutes at least.

I was in the kitchen when I heard the loud crash, much like a rifle shot. I was chilled to the bone. My heart almost stopped. I knew what that sound meant.

Running into the bedroom I found him lying on his back on the floor bleeding from a head wound. I was afraid to move him; his neck looked like it was in trouble. Filled with fear, I quickly called my neighbour, Art, for help. He stayed with Carl while I answered all the questions the 911 dispatcher had on her list, the procedure when making a call. Being tied up on the phone in the kitchen meant I couldn't be in the bedroom with Carl if he needed help. Quickly telling them what the emergency was doesn't do the trick. There are many questions they want answered before you're freed from the phone.

The boys came and loaded him up once more, transferring him to the emergency room. After x-rays, it was found that his neck wasn't broken; but the x-rays did show him having pneumonia in his lungs. He received six stitches to his head which left a sizeable knot on the back of his head, almost big enough to hold in my hand. He was in the emergency department all day until the doctor had the chance to drain him. It was six o'clock by then, and Carl said "NO" in plain English. After being poked and prodded and moved around during the day to three different rooms, he was going into a sundowning mode; when he reached this point, it was time to leave him alone.

Usually he was much better behaved, being on a little pill every night that kept him level and helped with the agitation that was common with this disease. Today was too much! Not being admitted, he was discharged, and once more the ambulance crew would be bringing him back home sick—having pneumonia, battered, bruised, and eighty years old!

The apron came off once again! I don't think it was ever to be put back on! I felt he was worthy of better treatment. Like he was worth something especially now at this stage of his life. I was angry!

Corina stayed with him while I rushed home to make his space clean and tidy. Since I had been at the hospital all day, the bedroom was still the way it was left—in a disastrous condition—a bloody mess (from the fall and head wound). This was upsetting to all…

I'm going to stop here for a minute and mention that Carl had health care girls who helped with his daily care as well as monitoring him. This included nurses who stopped by on a regular basis to ensure that all was well with him.

After bringing Carl back home once more and getting him settled, all was well until four o'clock in the morning when he was to go back to the hospital once more. After a restless night, with his head still oozing from the cut, he was to once again end up in the emergency room. This time he wouldn't be leaving until he had a drain inserted. Later, the doctor on call was to relieve the pressure on his abdomen, removing over five litres of fluid.

Once more Corina and I were holding his hands, keeping him in a happy place. The weight of that fluid was over fifteen pounds. That was a huge "baby" if you asked me. It would require a c-section for sure! Now, if you take his weight into consideration, it was quite a burden to carry around. This time he was admitted for one night. His weight was eighty-six pounds. The next morning when going to check on him I was told that he was discharged. I barely recognized him lying in the bed. He looked like a shell of the man I had left there. From what I could figure out, the excess fluid in his body had caused him to puff up, making him look like he had put on weight; but in actual fact, it was just fluid.

Disappointed, I was to take him home once more with the ambulance crew doing the honours again. That was his last time staying at the hospital or visiting the emergency department. Someone in the medical profession had informed me at that time that Carl probably wouldn't survive until Christmas. This news sent me into a depression. No matter what I did to keep him with us, it just wasn't going to work out for the best. I knew better. There is a "life sentence" that comes with Alzheimer's—I knew full well what it was, so… I should have known better.

After seeing him, his private nurse, Carla, said, "No, he is not dying; he is suffering from a concussion." He was too ill to join us for Christmas, but he did recover. Carla removed his stitches. We kept him comfortable; he had his own Christmas tree and Santa brought him some gifts that would become his favourites. One of them was an electric blanket to keep him warm—just what he needed. His granddaughters kept him company on his bed. Jaycelin read to him just as he once read story books to them. No, their Grandpa was never left alone in his recovery during this dark period of my life.

Jaycelin once approached me and said, "I don't think Grandpa is getting enough to eat." No, he wasn't, but he was at a stage where it wasn't easy trying to feed him; his responsiveness wasn't allowing me to. It was a period that was the darkest, with him slowly recovering. He was bedridden at this point, never walking again.

Jennifer, his home-care worker, was our rock during this trying time. They shared a special bond. Whenever she stepped into the bedroom, his face lit up. Like Jaycelin had remarked years before, he had the look of love on his face, and Jennifer likewise. Between us we set him up with safety rails on each side of the bed, just in case he got a spurt of energy from somewhere beyond and decided to go on another adventure.

He was a happy camper at this time: being in his own bed, Jaycelin and Kharis keeping him company, Jennifer paying him visits, all his favourites to eat and drink, and most of all, being surrounded by love. Jennifer always took a few extra minutes to sit with him beside his bed, holding his hands and talking. Before she left him, she had a routine of putting lip balm on him and getting him to smack his lips. This was their routine at the end of each of her visits. Somewhat similar to me teaching him to burp after each drink. He was always happy after her visits.

She also set him up with a TV set in his room. Now he could enjoy some movies. His favourite was Johnny Cash; another was an old-style country music movie with Hank Williams when he started out on his path to stardom. There were also some westerns that he was fond of. We also had him set up with a CD player. Now he could listen to his favourite country music greats.

Yes, he was happy, and enjoyed all the attention from those who cared about him. Jennifer had a friend, Denise, who was also involved in Carl's home care. He was to grow fond of her as well, enjoying the friendly bantering between them. He once told one of the two that he was going to put her down a hole, but he thought that she was too skinny.

After his last big fall and long recovery, he was on the mend and more alert and conscious then he had been since he was diagnosed with Alzheimer's. Is it possible that the nasty bang on his head had jarred something in his brain? Put something back together again? Back where it should have been? I was curious about this for a long while.

One day, after one of his sweet cravings, he told the two girls how to make date squares. The last bit of information regarding how to make them was to cut them into squares. This was good for someone suffering from memory loss! If he would keep remembering the good things in life, all would be okay. He enjoyed talking, still mentioning his friends from childhood days.

An event that bothered him through the years was the fact that someone had broken into his childhood home after his father had passed away. There were many treasured items, even the contents of family treasures in a trunk no longer there. The chairs from his mother's table were missing. The beautiful table was left behind, so Carl locked it in the garage along with the old-fashioned railing from the stairs which he had removed and put with the table for safe keeping. He was planning on using this in our home. Someone out there had some ill-gotten family treasures that were dear to his heart.

Who had the "balls" to do this? (I hope you don't mind my choice of words. I picked up a few of them over the years from being with Carl. Every once in a while I fish one out of my memory bank and use it when I want to pack a punch. Not just a little tap, but a solid punch. Oh, by the way...this particular word is in the dictionary. I checked.)

Now that he was confined to his bed, Carl wasn't able to enjoy the shower that he once welcomed. Every day I would give him a bath in his bed, never forgetting his Old Spice. He also had a rub down with his Vaseline Intensive Care Lotion to keep his skin smooth and healthy. He enjoyed this as much as his bath. One morning after rubbing the lotion onto his legs, he told me that I was a "smart girl." This was his way of saying thank you.

Speaking of his Old Spice, I could never get enough of it. I always enjoyed the scent coming from Carl after this part of his care and would tend to use a bit more than necessary. It would be nice if someone were to invent an air freshener that a person could spray the air with to get the full effect. I also set up a barber shop of sorts when Carl was in need of a good trim, cutting his hair as he lay in bed. I would then hold a mirror up so he could check out the results and give me his approval.

His shaving had to be kept up. After a few "runs" with my nerves kicking in, I was to get quite good at it. Manning the razor and soaping up his face—it was a long way from the early days when I would enjoy watching him shave. There wasn't too much more I could do to keep him comfortable other than creating a miracle which would get him back up out of that bed and onto his feet again.

Oh, speaking of shaving, if I was to accidently nick his face and start a bleed, I had a remedy for that. I went to the corner store and bought a pack of rolling papers. This was the farmer's way of stopping the bleeding. They worked very well. I would just take a small piece of paper and apply it to the cut. All farmers who smoked used this method, I believe, and it worked great. Most of them smoked "roll-your-owns" so they had a supply of papers on hand. The paper was waterproof or something different which is most likely why it worked. Carl's health care workers smiled when they saw the papers sitting on the stand beside his bed and of course would tease us about them, not quite believing my story. He was to spend a good six to seven months in bed, so I was to become quite skilled at his bedside care, even able to change his bedding with him still in it.

After he was bedridden, Garfield paid him a visit, arriving early in the morning before eight o'clock. He lay on the bed beside Carl and their visit was filled with laughter. Just like the years long before when the two of them were good buddies and enjoying their life, trying to stay out of trouble in the meantime. The two friends had breakfast together in the bedroom. Garfield had bacon and eggs and Carl had scrambled eggs which he enjoyed and could still muster if I made them creamy for him. Garfield helped with the cooking, standing at the stove, keeping watch on the bacon.

This will be one of the memories that I shall always hold dear to my heart. Two childhood buddies getting together, sharing what was to be their last visit together. It was like yesterday, as if all the years that had passed between them didn't change their friendship. It was still strong as ever. They were still there for each other, still caring.

With Carl lying in bed, it was a challenge when it came to feeding him. Now without his dentures, and unable to sit up, care had to be taken so he wouldn't choke while eating—although propping him up helped. It didn't help matters any with the fluid buildup in his belly, either. He would usually eat only two big meals: his breakfast and dinner with something light in between. Being on the safe side, all the food that I offered him was either very soft or mashed to protect him from choking.

From my jottings, I will share with you two days of his menus.

February 23, 2018

Breakfast: 2 boiled eggs, mashed

½ banana mashed & blueberry yogurt

Orange juice and water

Coffee – by demand

Butterscotch pudding

Lunch: Rice pudding

Orange juice and water

Dinner: Mashed potatoes with chives

And parsley.

Mashed carrots

Turkey Pot Pie (Mashed)

More orange juice

February 24, 2018

Breakfast: Scrambled eggs

Creamy with cheddar cheese

and salad fixings

Orange juice and water

Mashed banana, rice pudding

Lunch: One large pancake with

canned blueberries (ate all)

Dinner: Mashed potatoes, gravy

Mashed carrots

Mashed macaroni & cheese

(Didn't eat much)

Bedtime: pill with pear sauce

Two strawberry apple sauce cups

COMMENT: Wonderful stuff you made!

Bedtime: Pill with homemade apple pie filling,

mashed with ice cream.

COMMENT: Great stuff!

With his teddy-bear who hears all his stories.

Grandpa Carl wanting his jacket so he can escape!

Loving him and fighting back the tears.

Orange juice was beginning to be his juice of choice. It was interesting working with Carl and trying to keep his diet healthy and also easy to digest because of his tummy concern. There were to be only two vegetables in his diet: mashed carrots and mashed asparagus tips. Neither seemed to cause him discomfort, and he enjoyed them. One special meal of his was "Schneider's Tourtiere," or meat pie. He enjoyed this mashed with some of the crust along with mashed potatoes and gravy. Pork steak was another favourite, broiled in the roaster with onions and spices until it was very tender. The meat was pureed, and the juice was used for gravy. He enjoyed his desserts, asking for apple pie and ice cream one day. I made the apple pie for him and he enjoyed it mashed with ice cream, minus the outer rim of crust. Of course, he wanted date squares one day, telling the two homecare girls how to make them. Another request of his was biscuits—not getting any one day, he asked the following day, "What happened to my biscuits?" Yes, he enjoyed his food.

Sadly, by this time it was difficult to let him have what he wanted. Choking just wasn't going to happen if I had anything to say about it. One other favourite of his was Instant Apple and Cinnamon Quaker Oatmeal. I would cook it for a few minutes extra which made it creamier and easier to swallow. Some mornings, he would eat two packages. Even though he seemed to be getting lots to eat, he was gradually losing more weight. This, I thought, was most likely due to the fact that his liver was failing, causing havoc with his digestive system and not giving him the essential nutrition from his food.

CHAPTER EIGHTEEN

End of the Trail

After all of this writing, I'm not sure if I've mentioned that Carl asked me one day why he had to live in this room, meaning of course, the bedroom. This was a remark that saddened me. There just wasn't a way for me to change this. At this point in time, his skin was starting to rebel from lying in bed. No amount of lotion or turning him or use of the sheep skin that Carla had given him could stop this from happening.

But he still didn't lose his sense of humour; his smiles were as big as ever—bigger, I think, now that he could no longer wear his dentures. Yes, inside he was still the young handsome man who I had married all those many years ago. I guess you could say I was now the "old" lady if what the young rascal at the elevator in Duluth implied was true. Carl still hung onto his sense of humour through all of this.

For instance, I liked to sing and would occasionally burst into song, sometimes scaring myself, not thinking about what I was doing. Some of these melodies would be in earshot of Carl, and he would ask me what I said. I think he heard me loud and clear, he just wanted me to say, "I was singing." His remark was always the same: "Oh, that's what you call it!"

I once asked him if he had ever had his ears boxed. He laughed, with no comment. He was certainly heading in this direction if he kept up with his clever comments. It is time to get on to something more serious that I have been trying to avoid...Carl and his decline...

I enjoyed having him settled down in our bedroom, in our bed. I could lie beside him while he talked. I still reach out in the night to check if he's in bed or not before I realize he is no longer here. His passing left a large empty space in my life as well as in my heart. It's as if I no longer have a reason to cook or make pies. He was my biggest fan. My teammate.

I cooked and he would spring into action washing the dishes, helping me in any way that he could. If I was making apple pies, he peeled the apples while I got the crust ready. He also volunteered to peel the potatoes for me. Yes, he was a big help, always here to make the load lighter for me.

Corina and Jaycelin would spend as much time visiting Carl as possible. Jaycelin would sit on the bed beside him and do her homework, keeping him company, not wanting him to feel alone. Carl seemed to know all wasn't good, telling me when he was in one of his talking modes that he wished he could have done more for us. It took me a while to get him off this subject and change his mind. He certainly didn't have anything to fret about, that's for sure.

The day when he was doing his soul searching, Corina and Jaycelin were visiting and he was trying to comfort us. He knew he wasn't going to be in our lives much longer. A comment he made was that we were "going to be okay." We might hit a bump once in a while, but we would be OK. I knew in my heart that this was his good-bye to us. He knew how special he was to us and I hope that gave him some comfort on this difficult journey of his.

During the following days, he told me more than once that Kay (his deceased and closest sister) had been in the bedroom; he could see her and talk to her. Yes, his special angel was visiting him from beyond.

A few days later, his nephew Donnie Bolen from Stratton stopped by with his wife, Cynthia, to visit him. Donnie told me later that he couldn't believe how frail Carl was. Carl told him that he could no longer walk.

As I had mentioned, after his last fall, he seemed to get his memory back which was a miracle—a blessing for sure. One of the men he previously worked with in the bush stopped by for a visit as well. I could tell that he was visually upset from seeing Carl lying in bed, a former shell of himself. From the hardworking man he knew from a few years prior till now, there was such a big change. This friend was Maurice Chabot who would be a pallbearer and would speak about Carl and their working days together at his funeral service.

Unable to walk, Carl was giving me a new cause to worry: bed sores! They were beginning to make an appearance on his body caused by his constant lying in bed. They proved impossible to control and difficult to treat. A special cot-like bed was ordered for him from a health supply store. The mattress on this bed would inflate and deflate periodically. This was to relieve the pressure points on his body from being bed-ridden. It was set up in a different bedroom and was higher than a normal bed. It made bedside care much easier for the nurses.

The big drawback for me was that I was no longer able to lie beside him while he talked and held my hand, keeping him company. All I could do now was to stand at the bedside and rest my head beside him so he would feel comforted. My main goal at this point was to not let him think he was alone at this stage of his journey. I would keep him comforted and feeling loved. He never complained. His smile was just as big as ever. If he was ever in pain, he never let on.

This period of Carl's illness was to be the worst for me, seeing the changes that were gradually taking over this man I had married all those many years ago. He was a tender, gentle soul that I had spent a greater part of my time with while learning the lessons of life, our love growing stronger over the years.

I fought hard so he would not see my tears. He was getting so frail and my heart was breaking—it was most difficult to take it all in. His kindness never wavering, he never forgot to say he was thankful for all the care he was given. He was quick to show his appreciation for his bedside care along with his meals. Even though they were slowly changing, he still enjoyed them.

I had to ask myself, how was I going to keep moving forward without him in my life? Where would I find the strength to go on without his beautiful smile? Was I being selfish? There was just no way I could keep him with me. If the truth be told, I believe he was hanging on for as long as he could, not wanting us to be alone...God Bless You, Carl...

Over the years with Carl we never stopped treating each other with respect. We kept those early years alive, the ones in which we were just happy to be with each other. The memories of those Saturday night car rides down the lonely country roads from our years of dating are still precious. They will forever be dear to my heart. To keep that feeling alive is special even if your hair is changing color, your back may ache a bit, along with body parts not wanting to work the way they should anymore. This is love. It was the kind Carl and I were fortunate to have throughout our days of being together, the kind Reverend Fairbrother knew we were going to have.

———⁓ᵐᵒᵒᵉᵗᵒᵒᵗᵉᵒᵒᵐᵐ———

We said our good-byes to Carl on May 16, 2018. During the evening, Jaycelin was with him setting up to begin her homework at his bedside. She enjoyed keeping him company and he was content with her being beside him. I believe he waited for his young granddaughter; this was a special moment just between the two of them after all the precious time they had spent together in her younger years. Jaycelin was very fortunate to get to know him, a kind and gentle man. The angels came for him that evening...

Dean, Carla, and their children came right away and we were all together to say our good-byes. This was a heart-breaking time for us even though we realized that he had stayed with us for as long as possible, even surprising the medical professionals. His journey with this disease, once detected, lasted from December 2012 until May 16, 2018.

This was the young man whom I had admired all those many years ago, the man who I had married. He enjoyed his drive down the highway of life. My best friend...still holding my hand at the end.

As I am writing this with *Willie's Roadhouse* playing in the background. It is Saturday night and the *Grand Ole Opry* is in full swing. One of the guest singers this evening is Vince Gill. He just finished singing a favourite of mine—a perfect song called "Look at Us."

Look at us, after all these years together
Look at us, after all that we've been through
Look at us, still leaning on each other

If you want to see how true love should be, then just look at us
Look at you, still pretty as a picture
Look at me, still crazy over you
Look at us, still believing in forever
If you want to see how true love can be, just look at us.
In a hundred years from now, know without a doubt they'll all look back
*   and wonder how, we made it all work out.*
Chances are we'll go down in history
When they want to see how true love should be,
Then just look at us...

Vince Gill, I hope you don't mind me putting a few lines of your song in my writings about Carl. It is one of my favourites—so perfect.

I want to dedicate this song to Carl and our life together. It's a life we shared going back to the beginning when our hearts were young to what we have today, still loving and caring for each other. We mastered Alzheimer's, never giving up, and not letting it destroy us.

A personal tribute to my husband

Thank you, Carl, for taking a chance on choosing me, a young farm girl, for your wife. All the years we shared together have been an honour for me, a true inspiration to be a better person. You never stopped showing that "special something" which I noticed the first time I met you those many years ago.

Forever...my once in a lifetime,
Valerie

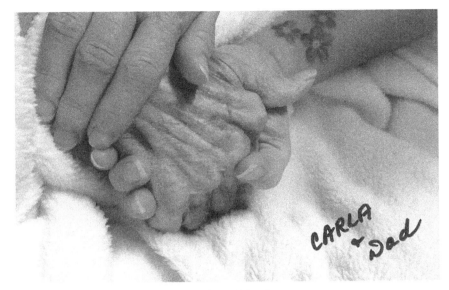

Carla and Dad

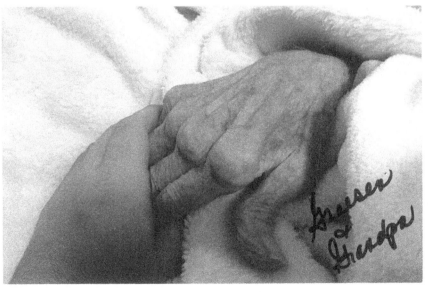

Graesen and Grandpa

Keighan and Grandpa

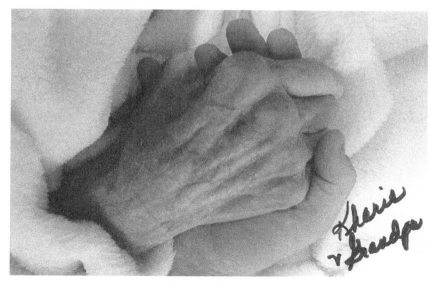

Kharis and Grandpa

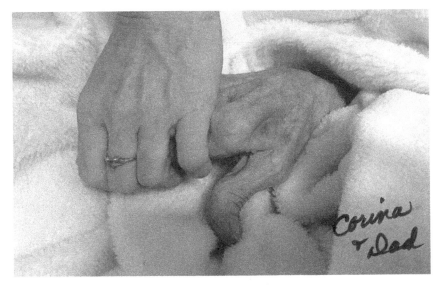

Corina and Dad

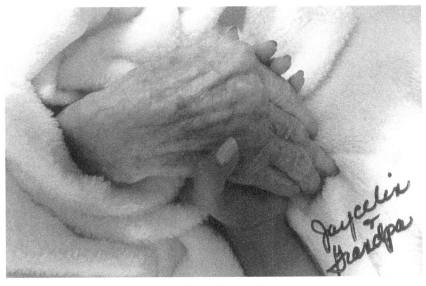

Jaycelin and Grandpa

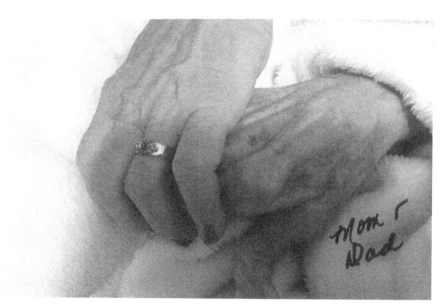

Carl and Valerie

EPILOGUE

Hugs From Heaven: A Fox and a Bird's Nest

An incident that was, to me, a visit from Carl, happened during the summer after his passing. A mother fox made herself a den on the Bolen's family farm where the house now has crumbled and fallen. Lilacs, crab-apple trees, plum and other shrubs from the family's farm life still thrive there and blossom each spring.

The fox gave birth to babies in this den. To feed them, she would go on a short run to my brother Phillip's farm and steal a young tender chicken for their dinner. From the early memories of the boys stealing chickens for their bedtime snack after the Blackhawk dances, to Carl looking out for his pet fox with the game leg, this recent story made my thoughts go out to Carl in heaven sending down his love.

Approximately two weeks after Carl passed away, I spotted something on our back lawn. On inspection, it turned out to be a bird's nest. The wind must have set it free from a branch. The surprising thing was that the nest contained a lock of Carl's hair! From shaking the cape over the railing after a haircut, a momma bird must have found this treasure and used it when making her nest. This was Carl sending down his love…reminding me of all the haircuts and conversations we shared over the years. Bless you, Carl.

Momma Fox and Babies

Birds Nest

EULOGY

This is the eulogy I wrote for Carl's funeral service, which I also read with my grandsons, Graesen and Keighan, and my brother Donnie to support me.

Today I am going to share with you some of the special memories that I have of Carl. He was a gentle man, with sparkling blue eyes and a beautiful smile. Even at the end, when his health was failing, he kept on smiling. He very seldom complained and took everything in stride.

He came from a large family, being the youngest boy with seven brothers and four sisters, so he was to enjoy lots of love and attention.

He was always small for his age. His sister Kay once told me that he wore size ten clothes when he was sixteen. He was the designated driver, chauffeuring his siblings to events and he had to sit on cushions to see out the windshield of the car. He also drove the ladies home from the Woman's Institute Meetings when they were held at the Bolen home. He was very proud of this honour and they would pay him twenty-five cents.

As a small boy he wanted a dog and he worked to buy himself one, who he called Mickey. Mickey proved to lack in good common sense or else he was an Irish sheep dog for he loved running and chasing cars. Like Carl he never gave up, losing an eye and a leg to this passion of his.

Carl enjoyed his life, growing up in Shenston, making great memories and good friends along the way. At the last he spoke often of the McKenzie family who lived close by. Their daughter Leone still lives in Stratton.

Another great friend was Garfield Faragher, here today, who he enjoyed growing up with and learning life lessons along the way—especially at the Black Hawk dances on a Saturday night. Their friendship continued on while working together for Mando Pulp and Paper Company. At one point they even had a motorcycle together, which Garfield sold before they seriously injured themselves.

One of them lost a shoe on one ride which was a serious event when you only own one pair. They had many fond memories of their growing up days and still laughed together over them.

At an early age, Carl drove himself to Rainy River for a driver's licence. Fibbing about his age to the licence issuer who was then to ask him how many miles he thought that he had driven. After Carl gave him a good figure, he said, "You must know how to drive then," and gave him his licence.

After nearly a four-year courtship (he took his time when making big decisions) we were married on September 17, 1965, in his childhood Lutheran Church in Shenston. By now it had been closed down but was re-opened and aired out for the big event.

He proved to be a good husband, always helping with chores. If he heard dishes rattling in the kitchen, he would come almost on the run offering to wash them. He usually dried them and put them away. He shared the task of making fresh apple pies. He peeled the apples while I made the crust. He often did the laundry down to the folding and even ironing what needed to be. Vacuuming was also a chore that he took upon himself to do.

He was the proud father of two girls. Carla was first born and then came Corina. He enjoyed this new role in his life and was one of the greatest, raising his girls in a gentle way, always there for them with advice when they wanted it, never critical.

He was the proudest of grandfathers to Carla's three children, Graesen, Keighan, and Kharis and to Corina's daughter, Jaycelin, whom he took an active role in raising when a young child and who grew very fond and attached to her Grandpa. He loved spoiling them all, enjoying going to their events and special occasions.

Outings were another favourite of his—whether it be on a little fishing trip up 622 or a trip to the blueberry patch. He even went on a hockey game of Keighan's in November, cozied up with blankets and in his chair.

One of Jaycelin's fond memories is going for walks with Grandpa and by the time they returned home his pockets would be heavy, full of pretty stones and rocks they would gather along the way. He would usually be carrying some pretty wildflowers as well.

Carl loved his country music, the good old-fashioned kind: Hank Williams, George Jones, all the great ones. He knew every singer and song they ever sang and spent countless hours making his cassettes so he could listen to them in his car.

Speaking of cars, this was another passion of his, buying his first new car when he was only eighteen years old. At that time, he was working in Atikokan. This was a 1956 Chev, and trying to get home to Stratton he was held up at the Pigeon River Crossing for three hours. They thought that he was too young to own a brand-new car and had stolen it.

He was a hard worker, and put great effort into always doing a good job. First at CAC, Steep Rock on the dredge, next on to Mando in the woodlands, then after a stint at Caland Ore, he went on to Great Lakes Paper, the first day they began their operation in the Huronian area. He spent his final 29 years here and operated every machine they brought into the bush. He was also used to train new workers. His final working days ended in Ignace when he turned sixty-five.

In 2013 Carl was diagnosed with Alzheimer's disease. This was to be the battle of all battles for him and he fought it with all the strength and courage he had, still with a smile on his face and never complaining.

If he ever suffered, he never let on. He was just happy to be at home with those whom he loved. As his health deteriorated and he was finally bedridden after he lost the ability to walk, he was gifted with homecare workers to help with his daily care. He graciously accepted this invasion, as long as they didn't touch him with cold hands. This is the one thing he would not tolerate, but they caught on quite fast. And yes, he had a favourite—Jennifer, who left him with a smile on his face after every visit. He once told her she was the best.

I am so grateful for that and all her visits, for seeing Carl smile was the greatest gift of all, which I shall never forget. They shared a special bond. His face always lit up when she came into the room. He was also very fond of Denise, who had such a gentle manner about her and could easily get him laughing.

I would like to thank you all for your compassion, your love, concern and all the support that you have shown to Carl and I over the course of his illness, for all the hugs and shoulders to cry on when things were looking bleak.

Suddenly I hear country music playing—it's Carl, happy in a better place now.

We will always love you, Carl.
... We won't forget...
Go rest high on that mountain
Son, your work on earth is done
Go to heaven a shouting
Love for the Father and Son.

A POEM

There is a very special garden,
Where the plants of memory grow
Nurtured by the kindness,
And the concern that loved ones show.

Roots are cherished memories,
Of good times in the past.
The branches tender promises,
That souls endure and last.

It is a place of peace and beauty,
Where bright new hopes can start.
Its memories lovely garden,
Soothes the hurting heart.

We gave out copies of this poem and packages of Forget-Me-Not flower seeds at Carl's funeral. The Forget-Me-Not flower is the official flower of the Alzheimer's Society.

Jaycelin Picture of the Forget me not flowers

FUNERAL SERVICE

Funeral services were held on May 22, 2018 at 1 pm at the Riverview United Church, Atikokan, Ontario. Pastor Dennis Schram, a brother to Valerie, officiated with interment in the Bolen family plot in the Barwick Cemetery. Pallbearers were Garfield Faragher, Philip Schram, Don Bolen Jr., Morley Bolen, Maurice Chabot, and Graesen Gerrie.

The Bolen family plot in the Barwick Cemetery contains five Bolen brothers: Norman, Raymond, Allan, Frankie, and Carl as well as Mr. and Mrs. Robert Bolen, aunts, uncles, cousins, and grandparents.

Carl's twin baby sisters were laid to rest in a graveyard west of the Bolen family farm. When trying to find their graves with Carl, we had no luck, being that the family of the gentleman who kept the records of the graves was stricken with tuberculosis and in controlling the disease, everything was burnt. This was common back in the early years before cures were to be found. This also happened to my grandmother when she was stricken with diphtheria. My father had told us that everything was immediately burnt.

Carl has one sibling left, a sister, Annie Armstrong, along with her husband, Melvin, living in a nursing home in Rainy River, Ontario.

ACKNOWLEDGMENTS

Writing a book has been a wish of mine for many years. I was never sure of a topic until Carl was stricken with Alzheimer's disease. Carl was fortunate to have such good care during the last months he spent at home bedridden. Thank you for showing the love and compassion that he deserved, for he had a heart of gold. The love and tender care you gave him left a smile on his face. This meant the world to me.

Many thanks to Nikita for being there for him and for your medical expertise when problems would arise—and for answering our concerns when we needed you. Also, thank you to Carl's special nurses—Susan, Christie, Kelly and Beverly—who were always available when we needed you, popping by to check and see how he was doing along with the bedside care you gave him.

A special thank you to Bev who would stop by daily to answer any concerns I had and to give Carl needed bedside care. She also spent the evening with us after he had passed away until Carl was taken from his home for the last time. Thank you, Bev, for readying him for this journey and for all your love and hugs. You were our angel.

To the home care girls—Kathy, Monique, Patty, Danielle, Nancy, and of course, Jennifer and Denise—many blessings to you all. Thank you to the emerg nurses, Jill, Suzanne, Taylor, and Kelly who wouldn't let him leave without one of her shaves, keeping him looking his best. I won't forget her dancing in the kitchen in our home, either. Carl always loved his music and dancing. Thank you, Kelly, for putting that smile on his face. This was to be his last dance.

A special thank you to Liz who treated Carl so gently and with kindness, never causing him any stress when it was necessary to poke him with a needle. He trusted you, Liz—thank you!

I won't forget the help of the emergency care doctors in dealing with Carl on this journey of his with all of their expertise and their gentle hands…and of course their stubbornness, not giving up on him. Great work! Thank you for your commitment!

Robert, I want to thank you also! Your kind and gentle ways with Carl after a fall, making sure nothing was broken, put him at ease. Good work!

And of course, the paramedics! Priceless! You certainly deserve your paycheque, not only for what you do but for the professional way in which you do it. For all your love and kindness, and being so gentle with Carl, I can't thank you enough. One can tell that you love what you do; you certainly can be proud of yourselves. Thank you again!

A big thank you also to my neighbour "boys" for helping me with my outside chores through all of this. To Harvey and Art, a big hug! Thanks for making my load a lighter one. I couldn't have done it without you!

I cannot forget my family. Carla, our nurse, was always there for her father, helping in any way she could, answering my questions, keeping me free from worry. Her medical skill was a blessing, with her Daddy on this journey. My trusted mentor! And Corina, always available at my beck and call on those trips to the emergency department…on our personal "speedway" trip to Thunder Bay. The many calls I made to her "crying out" when needing someone by my side, gripping her Daddy's hands in the emergency room, keeping him calm. Carl loved you both and put his trust in you on this journey down this rabbit hole of ours in the darkness, while we waited to see the light at the end. Love you both, girls!

To our grandchildren who were there with us on this journey of Grandpa's, helping to make it easier, always caring and loving their Grandpa until the end—he was so proud of you! Love you to bits! Keep on doing what you love in life! Stand tall! Make a difference!

Thank you to my sisters, Sharon and Norma. I hope that I wasn't too much of a bother with my phone calls when I needed someone to talk to, when the road ahead would get gloomy. Thanks also, Norma, for the calls you made to Carl while I was still working, keeping his spirits up, giving him something to look forward to, brightening up his day. Also, Betty and Wendy, two more of my sisters, and my brother, Leslie: thank you for thinking of us and caring in our time of need—love you all!

My sister, Faye, who was always there for me, encouraging me, listening to my worries, and keeping my spirits up to finish this story, and her granddaughter, Olivia Rose, who left the note of love for Carl: you are so precious. Take care of your Grandpa. I will always remember what you once said to him. "I love you just the way you are." Your Grandpa and Grandma are so lucky to have you in their lives to enjoy.

Garfield, I can't forget you either—the handmade cross you created for him out of birch, so dear to my heart. It is set up at the back of my garden with forget-me-nots blossoming around it. Also, the caring call you made on Christmas day from you and Judy…precious!

To my neighbour, Art Skinner, for his tribute in Carl's memory: a stand for his water pump from the Bolen family farm so that it can be displayed and have a place of honour. I can just imagine all the fun Carl had swinging on that pump handle, getting fresh water for his Mom.

And to Norman McQuaker for lending me your grey sweatshirt those many years ago in 1962, I think, which would be fifty-eight years. This was to be my first outing with Carl, and it lasted until he passed away in May 2018. Thanks for lending me the shirt off your back!

Thanks, also, to Carl's childhood friend Leone, a sister to Clarence McKenzie, who was kind in sharing her brother's story during the war and giving me his photo for this book.

A big thank you to Judy Watts for doing the time-consuming task of taking my handwritten words and putting them into type. And then the technical editing of organizing the chapters and paragraphs—our very first edit! Great job! Not an easy feat, reading what someone has handwritten and trying to decipher it. Well done! Thank you.

To my friend, Cherie Carpenter, who never gave up on me, even when I doubted myself, offering encouragement to keep me going with my writing. Thank you for all you have done—for the many calls I made when my confidence would begin to waver. Thank you! You had the knack for boosting me up and getting me back on track! Also, I won't forget the countless hours you spent assisting me with editing my writing. Thank you for offering me your time and expert advice! It was a blessing to have a "new set of eyes" reading my works. You truly made my first story (a time-consuming endeavour) come to life! Thank you! Special thank you to Gary Gingras for photo restorations, his kindness and very helpful nature.

A special tribute to my long-time friend Winnie Skrenski who lost her struggle with cancer on March 20.2020 at the age of 69. I will always cherish our special memories.

I have been richly blessed by all those who have touched my life in some way during this journey of Carl's and for the new friendships that I have made along the way.

Love you all!

Appendix I: CARL'S FAVOURITE RECIPES

CARL'S FAVOURITE BISCUITS

3 cups flour
3 tbsp sugar
1 tsp salt
2 tbsp baking powder (rounded)
2/3 tsp cream of tarter
¾ cup cold butter
1 cup cold milk

Mix dry ingredients in bowl.

Cut in butter until crumbly.

Pour in milk. Stir quickly to make soft dough (you may need to add a bit more milk, depending on your flour).

Handle only until dough is soft and then turn out onto floured board. Pat into desired thickness, at least half as thick as you would like your biscuits. Cut out with small cookie cutter and place on cookie sheet covered with parchment paper. Bake at 450 degrees for 12 to 15 minutes.

You can substitute ¼ of the cold butter for grated cheddar cheese.

Note: You can also place the biscuits on top of beef stew and bake.

Very good!

OLD FASHIONED BUTTER TARTS

¾ cup butter or margarine
1 lb brown sugar (3 to 4 cups)
3 eggs
Dash salt
2 tsp Vanilla
1 c milk (2% or whole)
About 3 cups raisins

Mix the butter, brown sugar, and beaten eggs together. Add salt, vanilla, milk, and raisins. (I heat this mixture gently on stove top to melt the butter.)

Use your favourite pastry recipe or you can try mine.

6 c flour
3 tbs white sugar
1 tsp salt

Cut in ½ lb Crisco shortening along with ½ lb butter until you have fine crumbs. Add about 1 ½ cups water and work in until able to roll out. You can add extra water. Take care not to add too much.

Bake tarts at 350 degrees. Makes at least 3 dozen.

DATE SQUARES

2 ½ c flour
3 c rolled oats (I like to add large flake to the top crumb layer)
3 c packed brown sugar
2 tsp baking soda
1 tsp salt
2 c butter or margarine

Crumb mixture:

In a large bowl mix the dry ingredients together. Cut in butter until crumbly. Press half of mixture into a 9 x 13 pan (large half). (You may have enough to also make an 8 x 8 pan.)

Don't press too hard or the bottom of the squares may turn out like cement.

Filling:

1 ½ lb dates, cut up
¼ c lemon juice
Cover with water

Simmer on medium heat until dates are a mushy mixture. If it needs more water, add some. Make sure dates are a smooth consistency and not too moist or too dry. If you like extra dates, add more.

Spread over bottom crumbs and sprinkle on remaining crumbs. Be gentle— don't press them down too hard. Bake at 350 degrees for 30 minutes or longer until a nice brown colour.

Like Carl said, when cool, cut them into squares and enjoy.

CARL'S "FLAMINGO" EGGS

3 dozen eggs – boil to hard stage & shell
3 c vinegar
½ c water
1 ½ tsp salt
1 tsp peppercorns
2 tsp mixed spices
*Add a few extra whole cloves for flavour
Thinly sliced onion (if you want)

Boil eggs. To cool down, run cold water over them. This keeps their colour from getting dark. Mix vinegar, water, salt and spices together. You can put the spices in a cheesecloth bag. Boil gently for 10 min to release the flavour. Remove spice bag. Place boiled eggs into jars and add the vinegar mixture.

You should get about three quarts of pickled eggs which Carl made every Easter with his girls. These would be dyed pastel colours. He enjoyed scurrying around the kitchen when this project was on the go.

If you like, you can add thinly sliced onion to the jars of pickled eggs for an added punch. Hope you enjoy!

Carl and Valerie at Little Falls

A MESSAGE FROM BEYOND

Letter from Heaven

When tomorrow starts without me, and I am not here to see, if the sun should rise and find your eyes, filled with tears for me.

I wish so much you wouldn't cry, the way you did today, while thinking of the many things, we didn't get say.

I know how much you love me, as much as I love you, and each time you think of me, I know you'll miss me too.

When tomorrow starts without me, don't think we're far apart, for every time you think of me, I am right there in your heart.

ABOUT THE AUTHOR

Valerie is the second born of 12 children, raised back in the good old days on a farm in Stratton, Ontario. Running wild, free and barefoot throughout the fields. Getting new shoes when school started in the fall. She likes spring, gravel roads, gentle breezes, country music, the smell of lilacs, picking blueberries, the smell of fresh mown hay. She loves reading, gardening, and searching for wildflowers – the first wild flower to peek their head out in the spring. Cherishes good friends, love of family, hugs from grandchildren and her precious memories of Carl.

CPSIA information can be obtained
at www.ICGtesting.com
Printed in the USA
LVHW032324210720
661242LV00003B/575